CULTURES OF THE WORLD

Angola

Sean Sheehan and Jui Lin Yong

Marshall Cavendish
Benchmark
New York

PICTURE CREDITS
Cover: © Volkmar K. Wentzel/National Geographic/Getty Images
alt.TYPE/REUTERS: 67, 69, 86, 90, 98, 99, 108, 124, 127 • Bes Stock: 54, 60, 61, 64, 65, 74, 78, 92, 95, 101, 103, 111, 115, 126 • Corbis Inc.: 3, 33, 34, 35, 40, 52, 53, 55, 73, 76, 81, 82, 83, 85, 91, 109, 118, 120 • Getty Images: 14, 15, 23, 32, 37, 38, 39, 41, 44, 45, 49, 50, 51, 56, 58, 59, 63, 66, 75, 79, 110, 112, 116, 117, 119, 123, 125 • Hutchison Library: 7, 8, 9, 36, 43, 48, 70, 80, 88, 94, 102, 106 • Jason Laure: 19, 22, 24, 25, 29, 30, 31, 47, 68, 72, 84, 87, 93, 104, 105 • Lonely Planet Images: 18, 100 • Marisia Laure: 16, 17, 77, 122, 128 • National Geographic Images: 46, 57, 71, 107 • North Wind Picture Archives: 20, 21 • photolibrary: 1, 5, 6, 10, 11, 12, 13, 26, 27, 42, 62, 96, 130, 131 • Topham Picturepoint: 28

PRECEDING PAGE
A mother and child sit by their home in Luanda.

Publisher (U.S.): Michelle Bisson
Editors: Deborah Grahame, Mindy Pang
Copyreader: Tara Koellhoffer
Designers: Nancy Sabato, Rachel Chen
Cover picture researcher: Connie Gardner
Picture researcher: Thomas Khoo

Marshall Cavendish Benchmark
99 White Plains Road
Tarrytown, NY 10591
Website: www.marshallcavendish.us

© Times Media Private Limited 1999
© Marshall Cavendish International (Asia) Private Limited 2010
® "Cultures of the World" is a registered trademark of Times Publishing Limited.

Originated and designed by Times Media Private Limited
An imprint of Marshall Cavendish International (Asia) Private Limited
A member of Times Publishing Limited

Marshall Cavendish is a trademark of Times Publishing Limited.

All Internet sites were correct and accurate at the time of printing. All monetary figures in this publication are in U.S. dollars.

Library of Congress Cataloging-in-Publication Data
Hestler, Anna.
  Angola / by Sean Sheehan and Jui Lin Yong — 2nd ed.
      p. cm. — (Cultures of the world)
  Includes bibliographical references and index.
  Summary: "Provides comprehensive information on the geography, history,
    wildlife, governmental structure, economy, cultural diversity, peoples,
    religion, and culture of Angola"—Provided by publisher.
  ISBN 978-0-7614-4845-7
  1. Angola--Juvenile literature. I. Yong, Jui Lin. II. Title.
  DT1269.S54 2010
  967.3—dc22   2009021203

Printed in China
7 6 5 4 3 2 1

CONTENTS

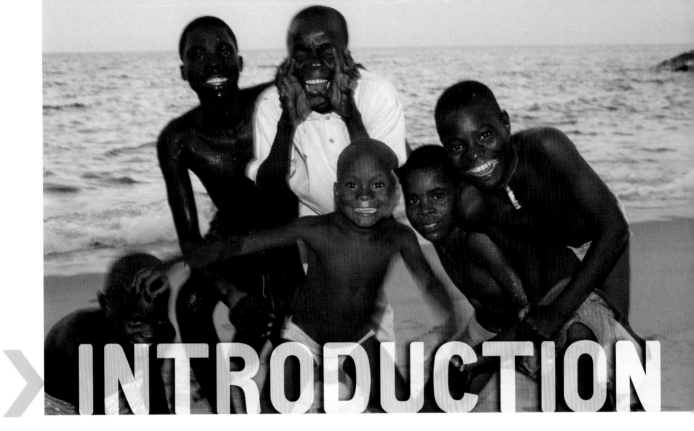

INTRODUCTION

AFTER MORE THAN TWO DECADES OF BLOODY civil war, the young African state of Angola is now in the hopeful process of rebuilding. The country is the second-largest petroleum and diamond producer in sub-Saharan Africa. With an area slightly less than twice the size of Texas, it is one of the poorest countries on the continent, but with rich natural resources such as oil and diamonds, it has the means and potential to become a prosperous modern state.

The country has developed its economy since it achieved political stability in 2002. However, it faces huge social and economic problems as a result of an almost continual state of conflict since 1961. The worst destruction and socioeconomic damage happened after the 1975 independence, during the years of civil war. Rapidly rising production and revenues from the oil sector have been the main driving forces behind the improvements in Angola's economy. But poverty is still widespread. Anti-corruption watchdog group Transparency International rated Angola one of the 10 most corrupt countries in the world in 2005.

GEOGRAPHY

A straight road brings locals through
the bushlands of Angola.

A NGOLA IS SITUATED IN west-central Africa and is roughly square in shape, with a total area of 481,354 square miles (1,246,700 square kilometers). Extending 793 miles (1,277 km) from north to south and 768 miles (1,236 km) from east to west, it is the second-largest country in sub-Saharan Africa. Angola is bordered by the Democratic Republic of the Congo (formerly Zaire) to the north and east, Namibia to the south, and Zambia to the east. To the west lies the Atlantic Ocean.

A small part of the country—the province of Cabinda—is physically separated from the rest of Angola by the Congo River. The Cabinda exclave (an exclave is an area of land that is part of another country but separated physically from that country) is a short distance north of the

The imposing Tundavala Gorge.

outlet of the Congo River, which forms part of Angola's northern border with the Democratic Republic of the Congo. The province of Cabinda is surrounded by the Democratic Republic of the Congo and Congo.

THE SHAPE OF THE LAND

Most of the country lies on a large plateau that, on average, is about 3,950 feet (1,200 m) above sea level. Some parts of the plateau rise to over 6,500 feet (2,000 m) above sea level. The highest points are Mount Moco, at 8,596 feet (2,620 m), and Mount Meco, just 121 feet (37 m) lower. Over time erosion by water and wind has shaped the plateau. Geographers call the plateau the "Great Escarpment" (an escarpment is a steep slope or cliff) to describe the effects of this erosion.

Along the coast is a lowland area. At its widest point it extends about 100 miles (160 km) inland. Between this lowland and the main plateau is an intermediate area, known as the sub-plateau, which is 14 miles (23 km) wide in the south and around 286 miles (460 km) wide in the north.

Angola's topography includes some very rugged and inhospitable landscapes.

Savannah-covered hillocks in Angola.

From the eastern side of this plain the land gradually rises toward the large plateau that occupies all but one-third of the country's total area. In places in the south of the country, however, the change from the sub-plateau to the plateau occurs abruptly, and there are dramatic escarpments of up to 3,280 feet (1,000 m) in height.

Nearly all of Angola's land is savannah—grassy plains with scattered trees. The Cabinda exclave has a small area of rain forest, and in the deep southwest, near the border with Namibia, is a stretch of desert. This desert is called the Moçâmedes Desert, and it forms the northern tip of the Namib Desert of Namibia.

From the Atlantic Ocean in the west, the desert gradually rises to a semiarid plain where African ironwood trees grow. Few people live in the desert; communities are found mainly in small fishing towns on the coast. The unique *tumboa* (*Welwitschia mirabilis*), a desert plant with a short, wide trunk and two gigantic leaves that can survive for about 100 years, is found in this desert.

THE *TUMBOA*

The tumboa (Welwitschia mirabilis) is one of the most unusual plants in the world. It grows in the coastal area to about 150 miles (241 km) inland and is found only in the Moçâmedes Desert in the south of Angola, near the border with Namibia. The tumboa has only two large leaves that grow throughout the life of the plant, which averages about 100 years.

The leaves grow to about 10 feet (3 m). Further growth is restricted because when the tips of the leaves drop downward and touch the hot sand, the leaves die. Because there is very little water in the desert, it is a mystery how the tumboa gets the water it needs to survive. The male and female flowers are carried in cones that grow in a ring above the leaves.

Fields of crops line the hills of this village near the Virunga Mountains in the Zaire province.

PROVINCES

Angola is divided into 18 provinces that range in size from the small exclave of Cabinda in the north, which is about 31 miles (50 km) wide and 93 miles (150 km) long, to the vast Kuando Kubango in the southeast, which is nearly 435 miles (700 km) wide.

Before gaining independence from Portugal in 1975, Angola had a flourishing tradition of family-based farming and was self-sufficient in all major food crops except wheat. The country exported coffee and corn (maize) as well as crops such as sisal, bananas, tobacco, and cassava. By the 1990s Angola was producing less than 1 percent of the volume of coffee it had produced in the early 1970s, while production of cotton, tobacco, and sugarcane had stopped almost entirely. Poor global market prices and lack of investment have severely limited the agricultural sector after independence. The Angolan civil war (1975—2002) and the consequent deterioration of the rural economy and neglect of the farming sector dealt the final blow to the country's agricultural productivity.

The town of Namibe on the southern coast receives fewer than 2 inches (5 cm) of rainfall annually.

The ever-serene Racana Falls sits in the Cunene province.

The northern region of the country, made up of the three provinces of Cabinda, Zaire, and Uíge, has a typical landscape of tropical savannah. There are also areas of woodland that are good for growing cash crops such as coffee, cotton, palm oil, and sugar. Fish, both in the rivers and offshore, are a rich resource. The tsetse fly—known for carrying disease—is common in the northern region, so raising cattle is uneconomical, as disease tends to spread to the cattle through the tsetse fly. In recent years, African farmers have tended to move away from chickens, beef, and dairy cattle toward goats and sheep.

To the south is a region centered around Luanda and its neighboring provinces. This is fairly rich agricultural land, with plenty of timber in Bengo province. The richest agricultural land, though, is found in the central highlands region that covers the provinces of Huambo, Bié, and Huíla. A variety of crops can be grown there, from corn and cassava to be eaten to coffee and tobacco to be sold for cash.

The two coastal provinces in the southwest, Benguela and Namibe, have a drier climate and do not support much agriculture, though some cattle are raised there. The inland provinces of Cunene and Kuando Kubango also have an arid climate that makes farming difficult; raising cattle is the main activity there. Finally there are the eastern, inland provinces of Moxico, Lunda Norte, and Lunda Sul. They are characterized by open countryside, and in the northeast, rich deposits of diamonds and other minerals.

FAUNA

Angola's rich animal life includes leopards, lions, hyenas, elephants, hippopotami, giraffes, zebras, buffaloes, antelopes, and monkeys. Birdlife and reptiles, such as crocodiles, are also common.

RIVERS

The three most important rivers in Angola are the Cuanza at 596 miles (960 km) long, the Cunene at 652 miles (1,050 km) long, and the Congo at 2,900

An Angola black and white colobus monkey carries her baby.

The Cunene River flows from the Angola highlands south to the border of Namibia. It is one of the few perennial rivers in the region.

miles (4,700 km) long, which forms part of the border with the Democratic Republic of the Congo. The Cuanza flows into the Atlantic Ocean about 40 miles (64 km) south of Luanda. Only the Cuanza and the Congo rivers are navigable for more than a short distance.

Several other rivers and their tributaries run across the country. Together the rivers form an important potential source of hydroelectric power. There are currently 15 working electrical hydropower stations in Angola.

CITIES

Luanda, on the northwest coast, is the capital of Angola. It is also the country's largest city, founded in the 16th century. Other important towns in the north are Cabinda, Soyo, Caxito, and Malanje. The most important urban centers in the central highlands are Huambo and Kuito. On the coast in the south, Benguela is the major town, followed by Namibe farther south. Other urban centers on the coast include Lobito and Tombua.

The inland population is small, and towns are located near sources of water, with Menongue being one of the few urban centers. In the eastern inland region the important towns are Luena, Saurimo, and Lucapa.

NATURAL RESOURCES

Angola is the second-largest petroleum producer in sub-Saharan Africa. The oil is mostly produced in the northern exclave of Cabinda, which accounts for about 65 percent of Angola's oil. In recent years substantial reserves of oil have also been found offshore, in both shallow and deep waters. Angola is now the eighth-largest producer of oil in the world.

Luanda is the capital and largest city in Angola. It lies along the northwest coast on the Atlantic Ocean. Founded by the Portuguese in 1575, it has a natural harbor and is a fine port.

Angola is also an important supplier of diamonds for the world market, producing nearly 13 million carats of diamonds every year. Angola's state-run diamond company (Endiama) has recently confirmed the existence of diamond and gold reserves in the southern Huila Province. Angola has large diamond reserves (estimated at 180 million carats), mainly in the provinces of Lunda Norte and Lunda Sul in the central and northeastern parts of the country. To date approximately 700 kimberlites, or rock formations containing diamond-forming peridotite, have been located in the country.

Angola also has substantial, largely untapped, deposits of minerals, including gold, iron ore, phosphates, manganese, copper, lead, quartz, marble, black granite, zinc, and numerous metals. Between 1950 and 1975 iron was extracted. The average amount of iron mined peaked at 5.7 million metric tons (5.2 million metric tons) per year between 1970 and 1974. With numerous powerful rivers crossing the country, Angola has tremendous potential for generating electricity. Angola currently generates more electricity than it needs. However, the sector suffers from war-torn infrastructure, and blackouts occur frequently.

A diamond mine in Lunda Norte province. The alluvial soil here is rich with diamonds.

THE UPS AND DOWNS OF OIL

Angola depends heavily on oil for economic survival. The country's current production is reaching 2 million barrels per day. Oil from Angola has increased so significantly that Angola is now China's biggest supplier of oil and is currently the seventh-largest exporter of petroleum to the United States. The most exciting news for the Angolan economy in recent years has been the discovery of massive new oil fields, most of which remain unexploited.

Much of the country's oil lies in the ocean, over 3,280 feet (1,000 m) deep in places, and it is only recently that advanced drilling techniques have been developed that can reach these deposits. Conservative estimates put Angola's oil reserves at around 10 billion barrels of oil. However, with the recent discovery of several new enormous offshore oil fields, figures as high as 20 billion barrels are being quoted. Angola is quite literally swimming in oil.

HISTORY

MWÊNE NJINGA MBANDE
SOBERANA DO NDONGO E DA MATAMBA
1582–1663

MONUMENTO EM HOMENAGEM
À SOBERANA NJINGA MBANDE,
INAUGURADO POR SUA EXCELÊNCIA
JOSÉ EDUARDO DOS SANTOS,
PRESIDENTE DA REPÚBLICA DE
ANGOLA E PATRONO DA FESA,
AOS 18 DE NOVEMBRO DE 2002,
EM ALUSÃO AO 27° ANIVERSÁRIO
DA INDEPENDÊNCIA DE ANGOLA.

* * *

COM O PATROCÍNIO DA FESA-
FUNDAÇÃO EDUARDO DOS SANTOS.

This monument at the main square of Luanda is dedicated
to the women who struggled for Angola's independence.

>>T HE HISTORY OF ANGOLA CAN BE
broadly divided into three stages:
early history, before the first arrival
of Europeans; the arrival of the Portuguese
in the 15th century and subsequent
developments; and more recent history,
with its tragic events and the present
status quo.

Popular Movement for the Liberation of Angola (MPLA) supporters in Luanda. The
MPLA dominates the Angolan government today.

Recent Angolan history, especially the years after independence in 1975, has been dominated by a civil war that has left hundreds of thousands of people dead and many more homeless.

The power struggle in the country was made worse by other, more powerful countries taking sides, hoping to use the Angolan civil war to achieve their own objectives. The United States, the Soviet Union, and South Africa armed and supported the different groups that they thought would support their own interests. But no one side managed to achieve complete victory, and the civil war took a heavy toll on the Angolan people.

Since the end of the civil war in 2002, Angola's economy has undergone a period of change, moving from the disarray caused by a quarter-century of war to being the second-fastest growing economy in Africa and one of the fastest in the world.

EARLY HISTORY

The land that is now Angola was inhabited from as early as 7000 B.C. by hunters and gatherers as well as settled communities of fishermen. The early

Typical village life more than a hundred years ago in northern Angola, near the Congo River.

hunter-gatherers, known variously as Bushmen, Khosian, or San, may have had a basic knowledge of how to make iron. Iron technology began in the Middle East and was introduced into North Africa by way of the Mediterranean. The art of smelting iron is believed to have worked its way down the west side of Africa around 300 B.C. through ancient trade routes across the Sahara Desert.

How and when farming and the use of iron tools developed in Angola and other parts of southern Africa is not known for sure. What is certain, however, is that the migration of Bantu-speaking people south to modern Angola had a decisive influence on future developments. The Bantu people, who probably came from what is now Cameroon (a country located in Central and West Africa) had an advanced knowledge of iron-making, which would have given them a great advantage over the Bushmen.

Ivory was a much sought-after trade commodity between the African kingdoms.

The migration of Bantu-speaking people into Angola may have begun as early as 1000 B.C., but it occurred gradually over time. There was also a later migration of Bantu speakers to Angola from eastern Africa. Much later, in the 14th century, another large movement of people to Angola took place. By the beginning of the 16th century nearly all of Angola was populated by Bantu speakers.

KINGDOM OF KONGO

Very little is known about the history of the region after the first arrival in southern Africa of Bantu-speaking people. As farming developed some family groups may have achieved positions of power based on their ownership

Early trade in Angola. Many Europeans were attracted to Angola and other African countries by the profits that could be made from trade with the local population.

Opposite: A family of slaves from Luanda. The man brings back a full basket of fish while the woman takes care of the children, the spinning, and the farming.

of cattle. This was probably the origin of the various kingdoms that arose after A.D. 1000. By A.D. 1200 the most powerful of these kingdoms was the kingdom of Kongo, which controlled a large area that included modern Angola. To the south of this kingdom a smaller kingdom known as the Ndongo kingdom, which stretched inland from Luanda as far as the Lucala River, also developed. Another kingdom, the Matamba kingdom, was based to the west of the Cuango River.

The Kongo kingdom's success was based on its people's skill in developing metal-working and pottery. The technique of weaving cloth from raffia palm became a sophisticated art, and Kongo cloth was traded as far west as the Atlantic coast in exchange for salt. The Kongo kingdom developed a currency based on seashells, which it also obtained in exchange for its cloth.

These kingdoms jealously guarded their territories, which were usually defined by the natural course of rivers. Sometimes they interacted with one another—in the first half of the 16th century both the Matamba and Ndongo kingdoms paid tribute to the mightier Kongo kingdom in recognition of its superior power.

SLAVERY

Slavery existed in Africa before the arrival of the Europeans. However, in terms of numbers, the organized transportation of slaves overseas, and the consequences for African society, nations such as Britain and Portugal completely transformed the activity. When the Portuguese first established themselves along the Cuanza River their main objective was to collect slaves. Over time this developed into a large-scale operation. Portugal's colony in Brazil, South America, needed a large number of slaves to work on the plantations. Between 1534 and the abolition of slavery in 1834, some 4 million Angolans were sent to South America.

However, the arrival of Portuguese explorers and traders in the late 15th century fundamentally affected all the kingdoms. At first they quarreled among themselves over the benefits they thought they could gain by dealing with the Portuguese. Eventually they united against the Europeans when they realized that the Portuguese were not merely interested in trade, but in enslaving them and taking away their freedom and their land.

LUNDA KINGDOM

There were also other powerful kingdoms besides the Kongo. One of the most important was the Lunda kingdom that developed in the 16th century. Lunda was a village-based kingdom whose people lived as farmers and supplemented their food supply by hunting and fishing. The leaders of this kingdom originated in an area southeast of the present-day Democratic Republic of the Congo and ruled through local chiefs who paid tribute to the king. The Lunda king was careful to appoint "advisors" in each of the chiefs' villages. These advisors ensured that the taxes that were due to him were collected.

Painting of Dom Vasco da Gama, an early Portuguese explorer. He was one of the most successful in the European age of discovery and the commander of the first ships to sail directly from Europe to India and then to Africa.

The Lunda king was given the title of *Mwata Yamvo* ("The Lord of Vipers"), and Lunda territory continued to grow in the 17th century. The people of the Lunda kingdom benefited from the planting of new crops from America that were acquired indirectly from the Portuguese. Corn was introduced in this way, and so was cassava, which was especially valued because of its ability to withstand periods of drought and still produce a good crop. With new food sources the Lunda empire expanded. Trade with the Portuguese developed, with ivory and slaves exchanged for guns and cloth.

THE PORTUGUESE

In the 1480s the Portuguese began to arrive on the shores of Angola. Their first contact was with the king of the Kongo, and early relations between the two groups were friendly. Both sides had something to offer, and mutual trade was easily established. The Kongo king was happy to exchange some of his slaves in return for the guns that the Portuguese brought with them.

The Ndongo kingdom was also eager to trade with the Europeans, and by the 1540s the Ndongo were dealing with the Portuguese, who had established a coastal trading post at Luanda. They even invited some of the Portuguese leaders to their capital, hoping to secure the best possible terms for future trade. This caused friction with the Kongo kingdom, who wanted to monopolize trade with the Europeans. Fighting broke out between the two African kingdoms. By 1557 the Ndongo had broken away from the Kongo completely.

By the 1570s the Portuguese decided to take over the territory. In 1575 the Portuguese landed in force at Luanda. The aim of the Portuguese was to conquer the interior, and in 1579 they were ready to move up the Cuanza River and attack the Ndongo capital.

COLONIZATION

The Ndongo resisted the advance of the invaders as best they could. It took the Portuguese four years to take land on either side of the Cuanza River and set up a second military base at Massangano. This would become the main interior post for the collection of slaves before they were brought downriver to the coast and shipped across the Atlantic to the Americas. The land they conquered was the beginning of what would later become the Portuguese colony of Angola.

The determination of the Portuguese to maintain a permanent presence in the region also brought them into conflict with the Matamba. The Kongo kingdom, too, changed its attitude toward the Europeans, and by the end of the 16th century all three African kingdoms had joined forces against the common enemy. Together they managed to stop the colonizing forces.

A sketch of a Portuguese hunter and his attendants with a crocodile in the late 19th century.

QUEEN NZINGA

In the early struggle against the colonizing Portuguese, Queen Nzinga (1582—1663) emerged as the leader most able to resist the advance of the Europeans. In 1624 she became the queen of the Ndongo kingdom. She had negotiated a treaty with the Portuguese a year earlier and was not prepared to let them overstep its terms.

When it became obvious that the slave-gathering Portuguese were not going to be bound by the treaty, Queen Nzinga retaliated by offering refuge to slaves who had escaped from Portuguese territory. Her willingness to encourage revolt among Africans led to a Portuguese attack.

In 1626 she was driven out by the Portuguese, who replaced her with a Ndongo ruler who was more willing to work with the Europeans. Nzinga, however, escaped to Matamba, where she became queen and continued to organize resistance. By 1635 she had developed an effective anti-Portuguese coalition and successfully contained their advance.

This success was due in no small part to a new female leader of the Ndongo kingdom named Nzinga. Under Nzinga the colonial advance was resisted and contained, but the Portuguese presence could not be removed entirely. A treaty was signed in 1684 and lasted until the middle of the 18th century. By then the Portuguese were ready to conquer more territory, and they mounted a successful invasion of Matamba territory.

A peaceful view of 19th-century Luanda.

During the 19th century the Portuguese strengthened their hold over the country and established cotton, rubber, and coffee plantations. Slavery had been abolished in 1834 on paper by the Portuguese, but forced labor was still widespread, so for the Angolans little had changed since the days of slavery. By 1920 the country was declared "pacified" by the Portuguese, with all effective resistance over. The country was now a full-fledged colony with a civil administration.

INDEPENDENCE MOVEMENTS

In the 1950s Portuguese settlers began to take over the best farmland and expel the Africans who had been working the land. Angolans were forced to work on Portuguese plantations. It was under these conditions that nationalist sentiment in Angola began to develop. The first movement to emerge was the Popular Movement for the Liberation of Angola (MPLA). By the 1960s it had developed a guerrilla force and was receiving aid from the Soviet Union.

The second movement to emerge was the National Front for the Liberation of Angola (FNLA), which was based in the Democratic Republic of the Congo (called Zaire at the time) and received aid from the United States. Later, in 1966, a splinter group from the FNLA formed the National Union for the Total Independence of Angola (UNITA).

THE END OF COLONIAL RULE

In 1912 the first diamond mines were established in Angola by the Portuguese.

Before independence was achieved in 1975 there was terrible loss of life in Angola. Hundreds of Portuguese settlers were killed and 20,000 Angolans lost their lives.

The Portuguese colony of Angola came to an end as a result of a coup in Portugal in 1974 that overthrew the country's military government. The new government intended to disown its overseas colonies, because maintaining control over these colonies was consuming a crippling 40 percent of the Portuguese national budget, and independence was granted to Angola in 1975. By the end of 1975, 300,000 Portuguese had left Angola; many deliberately destroyed factories and plantations before they left.

Unfortunately independence was only the beginning of a new chapter in Angola's struggle to survive. The three nationalist movements—MPLA, FNLA, and UNITA—began to jostle for power, and civil war broke out.

CIVIL WAR

The civil war that has been a feature of much of Angolan life since 1975 owes much to the international conflicts of the time. The United States supported the FNLA and UNITA because it saw the struggle as a way to contain Soviet influence in Africa. South Africa, on the other hand, viewed the struggle as a way to resist radical Black Nationalism. Black Nationalism advocates a racial definition (or redefinition) of black national identity, as opposed to multiculturalism.

Portuguese soldiers attempt to put down pro-independence guerrilla forces in 1961.

South Africa, which had its own colony of Namibia bordering Angola, wanted to prevent the MPLA from gaining victory because the MPLA supported the Namibian struggle for independence. These outside forces were already involved in Angola before independence was granted in 1975. In 1975 Cuba joined the conflict and sent troops to support the MPLA against South African troops that had invaded from the south.

Most Portuguese settlers fled Angola when the country gained independence in 1975.

AN UNEASY PEACE

The Angolan civil war dragged on through the 1980s. At one point the MPLA held the support of most of the population, but because of the MPLA's anticapitalist stand, the United States was determined to help UNITA defeat the MPLA militarily. This led to American support for a second South African invasion in 1981. However, South Africa withdrew from the conflict at the end of the 1980s. This was followed by the withdrawal of Cuban troops. With the collapse of the Soviet Union in the early 1990s, Soviet support for the MPLA stopped. The MPLA then began to shed its belief in Soviet-style economics and one-party rule.

A treaty was signed in 1991 between the MPLA and UNITA, and a new order seemed to be emerging, with the promise of free elections and free speech. However, there was a return to civil war when UNITA, unhappy at losing the elections that took place in 1992, took up arms again. Another

Angola's representative Afonso Van-Dunem addresses the assembly at United Nations headquarters in New York in 1988.

peace treaty, the Lusaka Protocol, was signed in 1994, with the United Nations taking on the task of monitoring the ceasefire. Unfortunately mutual distrust between the MPLA and UNITA, coupled with loose international monitoring, led to the collapse of the protocol. Both sides continued to build up their stockpile of arms and the United Nations Security Council delayed full deployment of a significant peacekeeping force in the area until late 1996. However, by December 1995 the government and UNITA were again in a state of war.

In 1998 the Angolan president, José Eduardo dos Santos asked the United Nations peacekeepers to leave, and in February 1999 they withdrew from Angola. UNITA's success in mining diamonds and selling them abroad at inflated prices allowed the war to continue even as the movement's support in the Western world and among the local populace withered away. Executive Outcomes (EO), a private military company, played a major role in turning the tide for the MPLA. One U.S. defense expert called the EO the "best 50 or 60 million dollars the Angolan government ever spent." Executive Outcomes trained 4,000 to 5,000 troops and 30 pilots in combat in camps in Lunda Sul, Cabo Ledo, and Dondo.

The Angolan military found and killed Jonas Savimbi, the leader of UNITA, on February 22, 2002. After that the military commanders of UNITA and MPLA signed a memorandum of understanding, and UNITA's new leadership declared the rebel group a political party and officially demobilized its armed forces in August 2002. That same month the United Nations Security Council replaced the United Nations Office in Angola with the United Nations Mission in Angola—a larger, nonmilitary, political presence.

LEGACY OF WAR

The civil war spawned a disastrous humanitarian crisis in Angola, internally displacing 4.28 million people, one-third of Angola's population. The United Nations estimated in 2003 that 80 percent of Angolans lacked access to basic medical care, 60 percent lacked access to water, and 30 percent of Angolan

children would die before the age of 5, with an overall life expectancy for Angolans of less than 40 years of age. Human Rights Watch, an organization that works to defend and protect human rights, estimates that UNITA and the Angolan government employed more than 9,000 child soldiers during the war. Human rights analysts found 5,000 to 8,000 girls under the age of 12 married to UNITA militants. Some girls were ordered to forage for food for the troops. If the girls did not bring back enough food, as judged by their commander, then the girls were not allowed to eat. After victories UNITA commanders would be rewarded with women, who were often abused.

EXCLAVE OF CABINDA

With an area of approximately 2,800 square miles (7,283 square km), the northern Angolan province of Cabinda is unique because it is separated from the rest of the country by a 37-mile-wide (60-km-wide) strip of the Democratic Republic of the Congo along the lower Congo River. The exclave of Cabinda is best known for its oil, which has given it the nickname "the Kuwait of Africa." Since Angola achieved independence the territory of Cabinda has been a site where separatist guerrillas fight to oppose the government of Angola. One of the characteristics of the Cabindan independence movement is its constant fragmentation into smaller and smaller factions.

GOVERNMENT

An Angolan woman casts her ballot at a polling station in Cassequel in Luanda during the 2008 elections. More than 8 million Angolans voted to elect the parliament for the second time since independence in 1975.

I N 1997, WHEN MOBUTU SESE SEKO OF Zaire was overthrown and Zaire was renamed the Democratic Republic of the Congo, hopes for peace in Angola were rekindled. Mobutu had been a staunch supporter of UNITA. The new government, on the other hand, supported the MPLA-dominated government of Angola.

Angola's national anthem is "*O Patria nunca mais esqueceremos*" ("Oh Fatherland, never shall we forget").

In April 1997 UNITA joined the MPLA to form a new government, called the Government of Unity and National Reconciliation. A few months later the People's Assembly, which was first elected in 1992, began to function, and for the first time representatives from both parties sat together in the National Assembly.

Mobuto Sese Seko at a meeting with other African leaders about the Angola crisis, before he was overthrown.

But UNITA broke away from the Lusaka Protocol in 1998, claiming that the MPLA had violated it. The following year, in 1999, Angolan armed forces destroyed 80 percent of UNITA's militant wing and captured 15,000 tons of military equipment, essentially destroying UNITA as a conventional military force and forcing UNITA to return to more traditional guerrilla tactics. The Angolan civil war ended only after the death of Savimbi, who was killed in an ambush on February 22, 2002. His death shocked many Angolans, many of whom had grown up during the Angolan civil war and witnessed Savimbi's ability to successfully evade efforts by Soviet, Cuban, and Angolan troops to kill him.

Six weeks after Savimbi's death, in April 2002, UNITA agreed to a ceasefire with the government. Under an amnesty agreement, UNITA soldiers and their families—a total of about 350,000 people—were gathered in 33 demobilization camps under the Program for Social and Productive Reintegration of Demobilized and War Displaced People. In August 2002 UNITA officially gave up its armed wing and put all of its efforts into the development of its political party. Despite the ceasefire, deep political conflict between UNITA and the MPLA remains.

Soldiers stretch a piece of rope tied to a skull across the road to mark the roadblock at the Angolan military encampment. Over the last few decades, soldiers and guns have become the most potent form of power in Angola.

The current president of Angola is José Eduardo dos Santos. He is also the leader of the MPLA. He was born in 1942 into an Mbundu family. The son of a bricklayer, he joined the MPLA before he was 20 years old. He studied engineering in the Soviet Union, and when he returned to Angola, he joined the war of independence. He became president of the MPLA in 1979 and won the general election for president in 1992.

WHO RUNS ANGOLA?

Angola is a presidential republic, where the president is both head of state and head of government, and is in charge of a multiparty system. The head of state is a person who represents an independent state. The head of government is the chief officer of an executive branch of government. In a parliamentary system, they are often the same person. Executive power

THE COUNCIL OF MINISTERS

Political power is concentrated in the presidency. The executive branch of the government is made up of the president, the prime minister (currently Fernando da Piedade Dias dos Santos), and the council of ministers. The council of ministers, all of whom are government ministers and vice ministers, meets regularly to discuss policy issues. Governors of the 18 provinces are appointed by and serve at the pleasure of the president. The Constitutional Law of 1992 establishes the broad outlines of government structure and outlines the rights and duties of citizens. The legal system is based on Portuguese and customary law, but it is weak and fragmented. Courts operate in only 12 of more than 140 municipalities.

MPLA supporters campaign for the party in the 2008 elections.

is exercised by the government. Legislative power is vested in both the government and parliament. Government includes the political direction and control exercised over the actions of the citizens of a state. Parliament plays more of a law-making role in the state.

Angola changed from a one-party Marxist-Leninist system ruled by the MPLA to a formal multiparty democracy following the 1992 elections. President José Eduardo dos Santos won the first-round election with more than 49 percent of the vote, compared with Jonas Savimbi's 40 percent. In the next election, held in 2008 (long delayed due to the civil war), the MPLA won 81.64 percent of the vote and 191 out of 220 seats.

MPLA

MPLA stands for the *Movimento Popular de Libertação de Angola* (Popular Movement for the Liberation of Angola). Formed in 1956 under the leadership ofAntónio Agostinho Neto, it was the first political group to seek independence from Portugal. Support for the party came mainly from the Mbundu people, and the MPLA largely developed in Luanda and other large towns.

Both the MPLA and UNITA were nationalist parties that called for independence from Portugal, but there was an important political difference between the two groups. The MPLA was attracted to communism as an alternative to capitalism. UNITA, on the other hand, was seen as an anticommunist party. It was this crucial difference in political ideology that led the United States and South Africa to support UNITA, while communist Cuba and the former Soviet Union sided with the MPLA.

In the 1980s the MPLA developed into a tightly controlled party that sought to govern Angola through one-party rule. Corruption became common within the party, and people of Ovimbundu origin found it very difficult to obtain official positions, even if they were well qualified. In the early 1990s the MPLA abandoned its Marxist past in favor of democratic socialism and

UNITA party's Isaias Samakuva during the 2008 election campaign rally in Luanda.

Government soldiers ride atop an armored vehicle in Angola.

endorsed multiparty elections in the wake of a peace settlement with UNITA. Socialism favors a society characterized by equal opportunities for all people. Communism promotes the establishment of an equal, classless, stateless society based on common ownership. In 1983 the MPLA added *Partido do Trabalho* (Party of Labor) to its name and became the MPLA-PT. The MPLA-PT is currently a member of the Socialist International, a worldwide organization of democratic socialist, social democratic, socialist, and labour political parties

JONAS SAVIMBI

Jonas Savimbi, the founder of UNITA, was born in 1934. His father worked on railroads under the Portuguese, and this helped Savimbi attend both elementary and secondary school. Savimbi won a scholarship to study medicine in Portugal, and he gradually become more interested in politics. In 1966 he established UNITA and built up its support in eastern and southern Angola among the Ovimbundu people. When an MPLA government was established in 1975, Savimbi organized military resistance, and with substantial help from South Africa and the United States, UNITA launched a civil war.

Savimbi became the best-known figure in Angolan politics during the 1980s. His fluent English and support from the United States helped establish his presence on the international stage. After surviving more than a dozen assassination attempts, Savimbi was killed on February 22, 2002, in a battle with Angolan government troops. Six weeks after his death, a ceasefire between UNITA and the MPLA was signed, but Angola remains deeply divided politically between MPLA and UNITA supporters. Peaceful parliamentary elections in September 2008 resulted in an overwhelming majority of votes for the MPLA.

Angola's national flag consists of two colors in horizontal bands. The upper band is bright red and the lower one is black. The bright red band represents the blood that was shed by Angolans during colonial oppression, the national liberation struggle, and the defense of the country against external threats. The black band represents the African continent. In the center a composition in gold is formed by a segment of a cogwheel, a machete, and a star that symbolizes the country's wealth.

UNITA's leader. Jonas Savimbi.

The elections held on September 5, 2008, gave a resounding mandate to the MPLA government, which won 82 percent of the vote, while UNITA won 10 percent. Various other minor political parties won the rest of the vote. The MPLA government has been sensitive to charges that it was a government that did not allow political freedoms and the elections were a conscious effort to boost the MPLA's image as a party that supports electoral democracy. In 1992 Angola's first multiparty elections ended in disaster and plunged the nation back into civil war. In 2008 there was little of the violence that had marred Angola's previous election and UNITA's acceptance of the results clears the way for Angola's leadership to focus on crucially needed developmental initiatives to rebuild the country, which had been torn apart by deadly civil war.

ECONOMY

The National Bank of Angola in Luanda.

THE ECONOMY OF ANGOLA IS ONE of the fastest-growing economies in the world, but it is still recovering from the Angolan civil war that plagued Angola from independence in 1975 until 2002. Despite extensive oil and gas resources, diamonds, hydroelectric potential, and rich agricultural land, Angola remains poor, and one-third of the population relies on subsistence agriculture.

Since 2002, when the 27-year-long civil war ended, the country has worked to repair and improve its ravaged infrastructure and weakened political and social institutions.

A worker at a diamond mine.

Banco Nacional de Angola was established as Angola's central bank in late 1996 as part of governmental financial reforms.

Oil and gas are drilled at this station in Angola.

High international oil prices and rising oil production have led to strong economic growth in recent years, but corruption and public-sector mismanagement still exist, especially in the oil sector. Consumer inflation declined from 32.5 percent in 2000 to under 13 percent in 2008, resulting in a better standard of living for the Angolans.

Although Angola is now technically a middle-income country, 70 percent of its population still lives below the poverty line. Average life expectancy is just 41.7 years. Only 2.7 percent of new investment is for agriculture, and the disparity between those who have benefited from the boom and the majority of people, living on the land, who have not, can be seen by comparing average incomes in different parts of the country. The average per capita income in the capital, Luanda was $3,476 in 2009, whereas inland at Bié it was just $201 in 2008.

A NEW ECONOMY

The percentage of females age 16 and over who participate in the Angolan workforce is 45 percent. In the United States the percentage of females age 16 and over who participate in the workforce is 60 percent.

Since 1996 the government has sold dozens of small- and medium-sized businesses that were once owned and run by the central government to private companies. The production of coffee is an example of this change. After independence the coffee industry was taken over by the government and more than 30 different state-owned companies were formed. All these companies are now being sold to private investors.

In another important change, foreign banks are being invited to set up branches in Angola. Even Portuguese companies are returning to the country as private investors. The largest private investors in Angola (outside of the oil industry) are Portuguese. Exports from Portugal to Angola rose in 2007 by 39 percent. International banks, and construction companies are lining up to take advantage of Africa's mineral wealth, and Angola is a prime target. Europe's banks are opening lines of credit with Angola worth 1 billion Eurodollars (U.S. $1.329 billion). Brazil also opened credit lines of $1.3 billion in 2006.

Container loads being docked at Angola.

In addition to oil and diamonds, Angola is rich in agricultural land and was once a major exporter of coffee, sisal, cotton, sugar, and tobacco. This could have led to the development of a balanced and prosperous economy, but what has emerged so far has been very lopsided. Oil money is flowing into Angola, but there is no guarantee that it will be used for the public good. Its main effect at the moment is to strengthen those in power.

OIL PRODUCTION

With growing instability in the Middle East following the United States—led "war on terror," Africa has become increasingly important for global oil and natural gas supplies. Angola passed Nigeria in 2008 to become Africa's largest and the world's eighth-largest oil producer.

Angola is now producing more than 1.9 million barrels per day (bpd) of high-quality crude oil from onshore and nearshore fields. The oil sector produces more than half of Angola's gross domestic product (GDP) and 95 percent of its exports, and the government plans to expand this by developing

the country's ultra-deep offshore oil fields, located 4,921—9,843 feet (1,500—3,000 m) below the ocean. The government hopes this will add an estimated 500,000 bpd to the current oil output level. President José Eduardo dos Santos's decision to join the Organization of the Petroleum Exporting Countries (OPEC) in 2007 appears to be a sign that Angola is returning to the world stage following the end of its civil war. Angola also hopes to begin to export liquefied natural gas by 2012.

Diamond extraction is a laborious process carried out using industrial methods.

China's government secured a major stake in Angola's future oil production in 2004 after promising a $2 billion package of loans and aid, including funding for roads, railroads, bridges, schools, hospitals, and a fiber-optic network. In addition to oil, China's manufacturing sector has also created enormous demand for timber, aluminum, copper, nickel, iron ore, and diamonds, much of which it hopes to get from Africa—Angola being one of its main suppliers.

DIAMONDS

Angola is Africa's third-largest diamond producer, after Botswana and the Democratic Republic of the Congo. Angola's diamond production is controlled mainly by the state-owned *Empresa Nacional de Diamantes de Angola* (Endiama) and produces about 10.5 million carats each year. Some of the revenues from the sale of diamonds, which once helped fund the war between the government and the UNITA rebel movement, are being used to fund Endiama's expansion and exploration program to look for more diamond deposits. Poor infrastructure remains a barrier to a diamond exploration boom in the country, as does the threat of political instability.

AGRICULTURE

Agriculture in Angola has great potential. Angola has fertile soil, a favorable climate, and about 142 million acres (57.4 million hectares) of agricultural land (land that can be used to produce food), including more than 12.4 million acres (5 million ha) of arable land (land that can be used to grow crops). The agriculture of Angola is currently expanding due to the end of the Angolan civil war in 2002 and the growth of foreign investment in the sector. However, the return to productivity in rural areas has been difficult and slow so far. Large areas still cannot be cultivated because of the presence of land mines. Functioning infrastructure in rural areas is limited, and there are few incentives for people to return to farming, hence the mass migration to cities such as Luanda to find work. After the war, from 2003 to 2004, only 7.2 million acres (2.9 million ha) of the available agricultural land were cultivated.

Women harvest corn in Kuando Kubango.

Agriculture's contribution to GDP—including forestry and fisheries—has been about 8 percent. Yet two-thirds of the population still depends on agriculture for food and income. Subsistence agriculture provides the main livelihood for 85 percent of the population. About 80 percent of farmers throughout the country are smallholders. Smallholders farms are very small plots of land, with low agricultural productivity. In the last decade of the colonial period, Angola was a major African food exporter, but it now imports almost all its food. The war brought agricultural activities to a near standstill. Some efforts have been made to turn the situation around, notably in fisheries. Coffee production, although at only a fraction of its pre-1975 level, is sufficient for domestic needs and some exports.

MANUFACTURING

A worker at a beer factory in Angola.

Besides the oil sector, which has grown, industry in Angola moved backward for much of the last quarter of the 20th century. The economy's industrial capacity was looted, destroyed, or fell into disrepair during the civil war. Many factories closed down due to lack of local skill, the absence of spare parts, and dropping local demand. Today up to 90 percent of Angola's consumer goods are imported. Thanks to the arrival of big foreign investors in the oil and diamond industry and the end of the war, however, industry may eventually reach prewar levels. Angola's potential to develop and boost its economy through manufacturing is enormous. Light industry survived the war years in a variety of areas—including textiles and clothing, footwear, soaps and detergents, and paint. Angola also has the ability to manufacture foods such as soft drinks, bakery products, and beer. In 1999 the Coca-Cola Company built a $36 million bottling factory southeast of Luanda, and in 2008 South African breweries pledged $6 million for the construction of a second Coke plant in the southern town of Lubango. In March 2002 the Benguela sugar factory was opened after a $5 million Angolan government-financed restoration by an Anglo-American consortium.

One of the most successful industries to survive the ravages of the civil war is cement. Overseas companies have invested jointly with the Angolan government, and increasing profits show that there is great possibility for development. Until other light manufacturing industries become as successful, however, the country will be forced to import many products that it could easily make itself.

MINERALS

Once one of the country's major exports, iron ore was no longer mined in the late 1980s because of security and transportation problems. From the mid-1950s until 1975 iron ore was mined in Malanje, Bié, Huambo, and Huíla provinces, and production reached an average of 5.7 million tons (5.2 million metric tons) per year between 1970 and 1974. Now that the war is over Angola is proposing to reopen and expand the vast iron ore deposits of Cassinga and Cassala Kitungo, and several large multinational firms have shown interest. Angola is also rich in several other mineral resources, such as iron ore, phosphates, copper, bauxite, and uranium.

The wide harbor surrounding Luanda makes the place a fantastic port, which has contributed a lot to the success of Angola's growing economy.

LUANDA—THE ECONOMIC HEART OF ANGOLA

Luanda is the capital and the largest city of Angola. It is both Angola's chief seaport and administrative center. It has a population of about 4.8 million (2007 estimate). It is also the capital city of Luanda province. The city is currently undergoing a major reconstruction, with many large developments taking place that will change the cityscape significantly. Luanda has passed Tokyo to become the world's most expensive city.

During the civil war slums called *musseques* stretched for miles beyond Luanda's former city limits. This was also partly due to large-scale migration of civil war refugees from other parts of Angola. For decades Luanda's infrastructure did not expand enough to handle this massive increase in the city's population. After 2002, with the end of the civil war and high economic growth rates fueled by the wealth provided by the increasing oil and diamond

A new railroad being paved in Angola. Transportation is becoming much more efficient with the growing number of construction projects in Angola.

production, major reconstruction then started. Luanda has recently seen an increase in violent crime, particularly in the shantytowns that surround the urban core established during the colonial years. Major affordable housing is also being constructed by the government, to give a place to live to those who currently reside in slums that dominate the landscape of Luanda. A large Chinese firm has been given a contract to build most of the government housing in Luanda.

Luanda has an excellent natural harbor. Its chief exports are coffee, cotton, sugar, diamonds, iron, and salt. The city also has a thriving building industry—an effect of the nationwide economic boom that has been going on since 2002, when political stability returned with the end of the civil war. Economic growth is largely supported by oil extraction activities, although massive diversification in economic activities is taking place.

Luanda's railroad was completed by a Chinese firm in 2007, and the port of Luanda is expanding rapidly. Luanda's roads are undergoing massive reconstruction in order to relieve traffic congestion in the city. The city has also invested more money in a public bus system.

TRANSPORTATION

The Portuguese colonial rulers developed transportation networks in the country by building railways and roads to help move produce bound for Europe. The most important railroad line, known as the Benguela Railway, linked Angola with Zambia and the Democratic Republic of the Congo. It fell into disuse as a result of the civil war, but it has been repaired.

Travel on highways outside of towns and cities in Angola (and, in some cases, within towns and cities) is often not easy for those without four-wheel- drive vehicles. Although a reasonable road infrastructure has existed within Angola, the war took a toll on the road surfaces, leaving many with severe potholes and littered with broken asphalt. In many areas drivers have established alternate tracks to avoid the worst parts of the road surface, although careful attention must be paid to land mine warning markers by the side of the road.

The Angolan government has made plans to restore many of the country's roads. Companies are coming into the country from China and surrounding nations to help improve road surfaces. The road between Lubango and Namibe, for example, was completed in 2003 with funding from the European Union, and is now comparable to many European main routes. It is likely to take decades to complete Angola's road infrastructure.

A boom in construction will result in new ports for Luanda, Lobito, Cabinda, and Porto Amboim. The current port system cannot cope with the number of vessels arriving, and there are regularly 30 or so vessels moored offshore for weeks waiting to dock. Luanda's new airport, Quatro de Fevereiro International Airport, is a modern airport with 18 international airlines. It served 742,629 passengers in 2004.

Construction workers building the structure of a new business organization in Angola.

LAND MINE CLEARANCE IN ANGOLA

The civil war created one of the world's most serious land mine legacies, threatening lives and causing the suffering of more than 70,000 survivors of land mine accidents. Militant forces laid approximately 15 million land mines by 2002. The problem is severe—over 154.4 square miles (400 square km) have been damaged by up to 4 million land mines, affecting 2.4 million people. The impact of land mines on agriculture, economic development, and voter registration has impeded national objectives. Several international nongovernmental organizations (NGOs) have made clearing minefields to protect local communities their focus, and the government has cooperated by destroying its own stockpile of land mines. But progress is slow. The head of the United Nations Development Program (UNDP) in Angola has stated that it will take 130 years to rid the country of the danger.

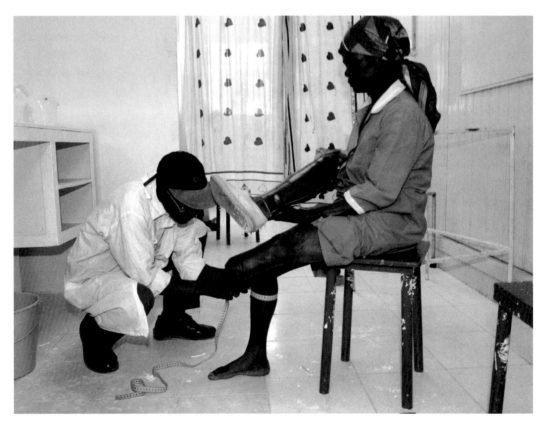

COMMERCIAL FISHING IN ANGOLA

The Angolan coastline is 1,025 miles (1,650 km) long, with two diverging currents (the Angola and Benguela currents) that create a strong upwelling system that supports vast marine resources. Fishing in Angola was a major and growing industry before independence from Portugal in 1975. In the early 1970s there were about 700 fishing boats, and the annual catch was more than 300,000 tons (272,155 metric tons). Including the catch of foreign fishing fleets in Angolan waters, the combined annual catch was estimated at more than 1 million tons (907,185 metric tons).

However, overfishing has contributed to significant reductions in resources. One-third of Angola's animal protein intake comes from fish, and most of the fish caught is sold within the country as demand outstrips supply. Fisheries contribute 3 percent of Angola's gross national product (GNP), and direct fish revenues are collected from the fees that the fishing vessels pay. Some of the foreign fishing fleets operating in Angolan waters are required by the government to land a portion of their catch at Angolan ports to increase the local supply of fish. Fishing agreements of this kind have been reached with the Soviet Union, which operated the largest number of boats in Angolan waters, as well as with Spain, Japan, and Italy. In other cases the government has allowed foreign fleets to export their entire catch in exchange for license fees.

ENVIRONMENT

Flamingoes in flight through a desert in Angola.

C RAMMED INTO ANGOLA'S GENEROUS BORDERS are many kinds of habitats: deserts in the southwest; arid savannahs in the south; mountains in the west, with associated afro-montane forests and grasslands; tropical lowland forest in the north and Cabinda; sub-montane forest along the escarpment; and vast areas of broad-leaved Miombo woodlands over most of the east.

A man walks through the garbage-strewn streets of a shantytown in Angola.

Epupa Falls lies on the Kunene River, on the border of Angola and Namibia. Such peaceful natural landscapes are under threat because of air and water pollution in Angola.

Population pressures and inadequate infrastructure have led to many environmental problems in Angola. Drinking water is scarce, especially in rural areas. Because food production has not kept pace with the country's rapid population growth, much of Angola's food must be imported. Poor agricultural practices have led to widespread soil erosion and desertification. Siltation of rivers and dams is a serious related problem. Deforestation, especially to supply the international tropical timber market, is rapidly eliminating the rain forests in the north and threatening biodiversity.

A protected area system of parks and nature reserves exists but lacks funding. Only about 10 percent of the land is protected on paper, and logging, poaching, and agricultural encroachment are continuing threats. The civil war caused tremendous damage and brought environmental programs to a halt.

Most of Angola is covered with dry woodland, savannah, and grassland. The total forest cover is 47.4 percent. Angola has signed agreements on law of the sea, biodiversity, climate change, and desertification. Soldiers are being trained as park wardens through an International Union for Conservation of Nature (IUCN)/ Ministry of Agriculture and Rural Development project. There are also extensive protected areas that remain relatively undisturbed.

DESERTIFICATION

The harvesting of wood for use as fuel also has contributed to the problem of desertification. *Desertification* refers to the loss of soil fertility and structure, making it hard for the land to support plant life. In Angola, forest areas are often cleared in order to harvest fuel wood for agricultural use. Traditional farming practices, which tend to be inefficient and land-intensive, significantly degrade scarce arable land—the single most important natural resource in Angola. Desertification can lead to downstream flooding, reduced water quality, and sedimentation in rivers and lakes. Because of all the dust produced during the desertification process, it also can lead to dust storms, air pollution, and health problems such as respiratory illnesses and allergies.

Beehive-shaped huts thatched with grass dot a scorched, scarred plain near the Moçâmedes Desert of Angola.

In March 2009
Cunene, Kuando
Kubango, Uige, and
Moxico provinces
were devastated
by floods, leav-
ing thousands of
people homeless,
dozens dead, and
causing a huge
amount of material
damage.

ENVIRONMENTAL EFFECTS OF DIAMOND MINING

At present the major environmental damage resulting from diamond mining is the diversion of rivers to allow for the mining of alluvial diamond deposits. After the mining is completed, the rivers are not redirected to their original course. This leads to pollution of the water and the destruction of flora and fauna. The mining activities also degrade the surrounding land by increasing atmospheric air pollution, contaminating surface and groundwater, and increasing soil erosion and leaching. The pollution, in the most extreme cases, leads to desertification and permanently changes land use from agriculture to waste, making it useless to traditional inhabitants in the long run, after the diamonds have all been mined. In the short run the inhabitants of the region are suffering from sickness and diseases related to contaminated drinking water supplies.

WATER POLLUTION IN ANGOLA

In some areas, the water is contaminated with raw sewage and industrial discharge from oil and mining operations. Safe drinking water is available to 46 percent of the urban population and only 22 percent of rural dwellers. Not surprisingly Angola's disease risk is among the worst in the world.

Sledging from the oil, gas, and diamond mines have caused water pollution in Angola.

WASTE TREATMENT AND DISPOSAL

Most of the country, including Luanda, has no basic infrastructure, such as water distribution and waste and water treatment. Residents bathe and drink from water that is thick with trash and waste from some of Luanda's bays. Without clean water, safe dwellings, and waste disposal, it will be difficult for the Angolans to address many of the challenges to their country's quality of life and education.

RECYCLING IN ANGOLA

Collect-A-Can, a recycling initiative that aims to reduce litter and save the environment, has set up a partnership with Coca-Cola in Angola. Collect-A-Can optimizes the cost-effective recovery of used beverage cans in the African region. Collectors form their own collection networks and deliver their cans direct to one of the company's branches, for which they receive top market-related prices. Angolans now can collect cans to exchange for cash in order to improve their lives.

Glass bottles waiting to be recycled. Glass makes up a large component of household and industrial waste due to its weight and density. The glass component in municipal waste is usually made up of bottles, broken glassware, light bulbs, and other items.

BIODIVERSITY IN ANGOLA

The exceptional biodiversity in Angola is due to the combination of a number of factors: the vast size of the country, its intertropical geographical location, the altitude variation, the biome types, and its 1,025-mile-(1,650-km-) long coastline. Biomes range from dense tropical forests to deserts. Of the estimated 5,000 plant species that are believed to exist in the country (without mentioning the vast floral wealth of Cabinda Province), 1,260 are native to Angola—making Angola the second-richest country in Africa in terms of endemic plants.

Giraffes roam freely in this Angolan National Park.

Angola's diversity of mammals is also one of the richest on the continent, with 275 recorded species. About 92 percent of the bird species of southern Africa occurs in Angola, with 872 known species. Angola is also an important center of marine biodiversity and a productive area in fish resources. Wide estuaries such as those of the Congo, Dande, Cuanza, and Cunene rivers support important food chains that are essential to the livelihood of the people that live there. Mangroves occur along the Angolan coastline and form ecosystems of important biological and ecological importance, providing harbors and nurseries for crustaceans and fish, and economic and tourist opportunities for the country.

A total of 120 plant species are listed as endangered, many of them occurring in protected areas. Trees such as the avicenia and combretum, which are important parts of the vegetation that protects the Angolan coast, are also listed as highly endangered species. Threats to biodiversity include uncontrolled bush burning to clear the land for agriculture, poaching of animals, logging, and illegal trade in animals.

BIRD LIFE

Angola has a bird list of more than 920 species, but there has been little ornithological activity for some 30 years. Angola has 14 endemic species of birds, including the gray-striped francolin and the red-crested turaco.

ENDANGERED SPECIES IN ANGOLA

Endangered species in Angola include the black-faced impala, three species of turtle (green, olive ridley, and leatherback), the giant sable antelope, the African slender-snouted (or long-snouted) crocodile, the african elephant, Vernay's climbing monkey, and the black rhinoceros. As of the late 1990s threatened species in Angola include 17 of the 276 species of mammals, 13 of the 765 species of birds, and 20 of the 5,185 species of plants.

It is common to see elephants roaming freely in the nature reserves of Angola.

Angola's Forest Development Institute (IDF) expects to plant 12,355 acres (5,000 ha) of trees per year from 2009. The goal is to fight desertification and deforestation in the country. The IDF reforested at least 1,260 acres (510 ha) in 2008 in Tômbwa (southwestern Namibe Province).

PLIGHT OF ANGOLA'S ELEPHANTS The bloody plight of the country's elephants is getting worse as a result of the illegal ivory trade. Unregulated domestic ivory markets in Africa lead to the killing of some 12,000 elephants each year. Within southern Africa, Angola and Mozambique have the largest illegal trade in elephant ivory. Angola's wild elephant population has not been surveyed for decades, and due to the lack of recent information, the International Union for the Conservation of Nature's African Elephant Database (AED) indicates that only 250 elephants are found in the country. Of the 37 countries that still have wild populations of African elephants, Angola is the only one that has not signed the Convention on International Trade in Endangered Species of Wild Fauna and Flora (CITES, which entered into force in 1975 and now has 175 member countries). In fact Angola is the only nation in sub-Saharan Africa that is not part of the convention, which serves as the world's main mechanism for regulating trade in endangered and threatened wildlife species.

CRITICALLY ENDANGERED: THE BLACK RHINOCEROS The black rhinoceros weighs 1,760 to 3,080 pounds (800 to 1,400 kg), and its height varies from 4.3 to 5.9 feet (1.3 to 1.8 m). The black rhino has two horns and poor eyesight, but its hearing is good. Black rhinos often have a mutually beneficial relationship with birds called "oxpeckers." The birds eat parasites found on the rhinos' skin and the birds' acute eyesight helps warn the rhinos

Once a thriving species, black rhinos are now very low in number due to poaching.

of potential danger. The black rhino is unpredictable and can be dangerous, sometimes charging when it comes across a disturbing sound or smell. Mortal combat is recorded to take place more often between black rhinos than any other mammal. It results in the death of about 50 percent of male black rhinos and 30 percent of females due to fight-related wounds.

The black rhino population suffered a huge reduction during the 20th century. In the early 1900s there were probably several hundred thousand rhinos; by the early 1990s there were fewer than 2,500. However, since 1995, numbers of black rhinos throughout Africa have started to increase again. Hunting and clearance of land for settlement and agriculture were the major reasons for the decline of black rhino populations in the 20th century. The situation facing the black rhino is still critical. The demand for rhino horn from Asia (for traditional medicines) and from the Middle East (for dagger handles) persists, and the threat of a return to large-scale poaching is still present.

GIANT SABLE ANTELOPE   The giant sable antelope, also known in Portuguese as the *Palanca Negra*, is a large, rare subspecies of sable antelope that is native to the region between the Cuango and Luando rivers in Angola. Both males and females have horns. In fact males and females are strikingly similar in appearance until they reach three years of age, when the males become darker and develop majestic horns. The horns are massive and more curved in males, reaching lengths of 2.7 to 5.4 feet (0.81 to 1.65 m), while females' horns are only 2 to 3.3 feet (61 to 102 cm) long. The male antelope weighs an average of 524.7 pounds (238 kg), with a height of 3.8 to 4.7 feet (116 to 142 cm). Females weigh 484 pounds (220 kg) and are slightly shorter than males. Like all antelopes they are shy by nature, but they can also be very aggressive. The males can be especially dangerous when they are hurt, attacked, or approached.

The giant sable antelope is greatly respected by the people of Angola. This may be one of the reasons the animals survived the long civil war. In African mythology, just like other antelopes, these creatures symbolize vivacity, speed, and beauty. The giant sable antelope is a national symbol of Angola and is portrayed on numerous stamps, banknotes, and even passports of the nation. The Angolan national football team is fondly known as the Palancas Negras in honor of the antelope.

NATIONAL PARKS AND RESERVES

Giant sable antelopes on the Luanda Rreserve.

CAMEIA NATIONAL PARK Cameia National Park is situated in the Moxico Province of Angola, located about 3,609 feet (1,100 m) above sea level. It shares its name with the nearby municipality of Cameia. The Cameia-Luacano Road forms the northern boundary of the park, with the Chifumage River forming the southern portion of the eastern boundary and the Lumege and Luena rivers forming the southwestern boundary. Much of the park consists of seasonally flooded plains that form part of the Zambezi River basin, with the northern half of the park draining into the Chifumage River. Two lakes, Lago ("lake" in Portuguese) Cameia and Lago Dilolo (the largest lake in Angola), lie outside the park boundaries. Both have extensive reedbeds and grassy swamps that are rich in aquatic birds. The wildlife was almost completely wiped out after the civil war, uncontrolled poaching, and the destruction of infrastructure devastated the park. There is a serious lack of staff, resources, and support for the park.

CANGANDALA NATIONAL PARK Cangandala National Park is a national park in Malanje Province. It is situated between the Cuije River and two unnamed deltas of the Cuanza River, with the towns of Culamagia and Techongolola found on the edges of the park. It is the smallest national park in Angola and covers an area of 231.6 square miles (600 square km). Cangandala was originally founded to protect the giant sable antelope, which was discovered in Cangandala in 1963.

A bradfields horn-bill sits in a nature reserve in Angola.

IONA NATIONAL PARK Iona National Park (*Parque Nacional do Iona* in Portuguese is a national park in Namibe Province. It is about 124 miles (200 km) (from the city of Namibe and, at 5,850 square miles (15,151 square km), the largest in the country. Before the Angolan civil war, Iona was an animal paradise, rich in big game. However, as is true for most Angolan national parks, illegal poaching and the destruction of infrastructure have caused considerable damage to the once rich park. The park is also known for unique flora and incredible rock formations.

QUIÇAMA NATIONAL PARK Quiçama National Park, also known as Kissama National Park, is the only functioning national park in all of Angola. The others remain in disrepair after the Angolan civil war. The park is approximately 43.5 miles (70 km) from Luanda, the Angolan capital. The park covers 4,633 square miles (12,000 square km)—more than twice the size of the U.S. state of Rhode Island.

The park once was home to many large game animals, such as elephants and giant sable antelopes, but after widescale poaching during 27 years of civil war, the animal population was virtually eliminated.

In 2001 the Kissama Foundation, a group of Angolans and South Africans, initiated Operation Noah's Ark to transport animals, especially elephants, from neighboring Botswana and South Africa to repopulate Kissama National Park. The animals adapted well to the move from overpopulated parks in their homes countries. Noah's Ark was the largest animal transplant of its kind in history, and has given the park momentum to be restored to its natural state.

Cabinda's most impressive natural resource is the Maiombe rain forest, described by locals as "the vegetable sea" due to its impenetrable canopy of green vegetation. The forest covers an enormous area, twice the size of some small African countries. Maiombe is often described as "the Amazon of Africa," hosting a remarkable variety of plant and animal species. Maiombe is especially famous for its butterflies (right). There are hundreds of species in the forest, many of them unique to the area. Prized by collectors, specimens of these butterflies can be found in natural history museums throughout the world. What is most beautiful about Maiombe is that the forest grows right down to the sea, with enormous trees bending into the water. Waves lap at the greenery as gorillas and chimpanzees swoop down from the high branches. However, Maiombe is not just an amazing paradise of animals, birds, insects, and vegetation. It also has enormous potential as a supplier of tropical hardwoods. There are many precious woods in the forest, including ebony and rare types of mahogany.

MUPA NATIONAL PARK Mupa National Park is in Angola's Cunene Province. It is significant for its wide variety of birdlife. Many Angolans reside within the park, which, along with nomadic pastoralists and mineral prospecting, threatens to destroy the park's birdlife.

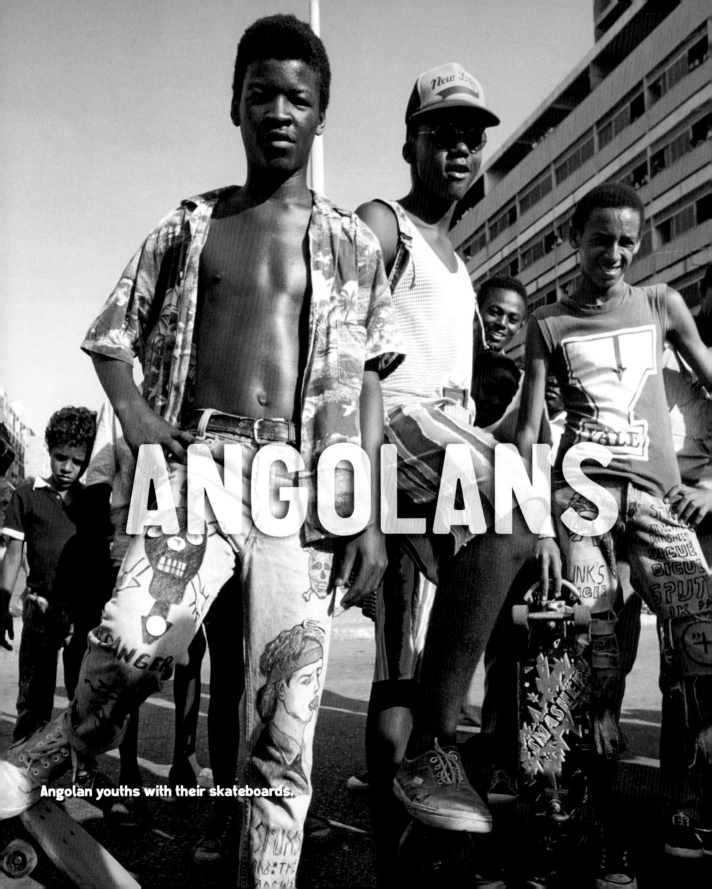

ANGOLANS

Angolan youths with their skateboards.

THE PRESENT POPULATION OF Angola is estimated to be 12.8 million. The birthrate is high compared with that of other developing countries in Africa. Women have an average of 6.2 children. However, given the size of the country, Angola still remains underpopulated, with an average of only 26 people per square mile (13 people per square km).

Mothers with their children. Angola's high birthrate means that young Angolans make up the majority of the population.

DIVIDING A NATION

In Angola a regional or tribal sense of identity is often more important than a national sense. Someone's sense of identity as an Ovimbundu may be far stronger and deeper than his or her sense of being an Angolan. There are historical reasons for this—the Portuguese never tried to create a sense of national identity, and after independence in 1975 the country was plunged into civil war, which pitted people against one another along ethnic lines.

Although the Portuguese did not adopt apartheid in the form it took in South Africa, Europeans were treated as superior to the native inhabitants of the country. Angolans—classified as "natives"—were only allowed to hold menial jobs. They were obliged by law to carry special *caderneta* ("KAD-er-ne-ta;" identity cards) that confirmed their status. As holders of the *caderneta*, Angolans were subject to special laws and regulations that limited their economic opportunities. In the 1950s only 5 percent of "native" children attended elementary or secondary school, and the vast majority of

The San live in the remote regions of the southern provinces.

older teenagers were unable to read or write. The only way for an Angolan to escape this fate was to learn Portuguese, turn his or her back on traditional culture, and apply for the special status of *assimilado* ("ass-sim-ill-AD-o").

This was what many people of mixed African and European ancestry did. By the 1970s there were about 30 Angolans of mixed blood for every 100 white Portuguese. Because most Portuguese colonists were male, those of mixed descent were likely to have a black mother and a white father. In practice this also meant that these Angolans of mixed race tended to identify themselves with the white Portuguese rather than with the black majority.

Crowds of Angolans gathering to watch their national soccer team in action. Sports serve to bring the different ethnic groups of Angola together.

ETHNIC GROUPS

Angolans are members of various ethnic groups, and these groups tend to be concentrated in different parts of the country. Each group has its own language and shares a sense of common descent and a separate history—this is what works against a sense of national identity.

A member of the
Ovimbundu tribe.

The largest ethnic group is the Ovimbundu, which makes up about 37 percent of the population and lives mainly in the central highland areas, covering the provinces of Huambo, Bié, Benguela, and northern Huíla. The most important subgroups of the Ovimbundu are the Bailundu, Bieno, Dombe, Ganda, and Wambu. The Ovimbundu were important long-distance traders in the past, and although trade is still a traditional means of livelihood, most Ovimbundu people now engage in agriculture.

The next largest ethnic group, which represents about one in four Angolans, is the Mbundu people. There are three major subgroups—the Mbaka, the Ndongo, and the Dembos. The Mbundu traditionally inhabit Luanda province, which includes the capital city. They have been exposed to the influence of the Portuguese more than any other ethnic group.

The people living in the northwest provinces of Zaire and Uíge belong mostly to the Bakongo group that is also found in the neighboring countries of Congo and the Democratic Republic of the Congo. In Angola they make up about 13 percent of the population. The main subgroups of the Bakongo group are the Bashikongo, Sosso, Pombo, Sonongo, and Zombo. Other groups include the Chokwe (or Lunda), Ganguela, Nhaneca-Humbe, Ambo, Herero, and Xindunga. In addition, mixed race—European and African—people amount to about 2 percent, with a small (1 percent) population of whites, mainly ethnically Portuguese.

CHOKWE

The Chokwe, a branch of the Lunda-Chokwe ethnic group, originally came from a highland region about 300 miles (483 km) southeast of Luanda. They were hunters, and when the Portuguese arrived they began to collect ivory and beeswax to exchange for guns with the Portuguese. They formed groups up to a thousand strong and began to expand their territory to collect more ivory and beeswax. In this way they spread both to the north and to the east. In the 19th century, by which time there were few elephants left to hunt, the Chokwe became involved in the production of rubber because of the increasing European demand for this material. Chokwe women became adept at collecting the sap from the rubber trees that produced latex and rolling it into large hardened lumps that could be easily carried to the nearest trading post.

THE PORTUGUESE

Given that the Portuguese were in Angola for nearly 500 years, one might think that a significant proportion of Angolans would be of Portuguese descent, but this is not the case. The history of colonial rule explains this, in large part. Although the Portuguese first arrived in 1480, it was not until the 19th century that they established themselves in the plateau region of the interior. It was only in 1880 that northern Angola officially became a part of their colony.

For most of their 500 years in the area, the Portuguese who lived in Angola tended to remain in a small number of coastal settlements. Even by 1940 there were only some 40,000 Portuguese living in Angola. By 1975, when independence was won, there were 340,000 Portuguese in Angola. As the war of independence escalated in the 1970s, an increasing number

A group of Portuguese settlers.

Dispossessed families take refuge in an open field in Angola.

of Portuguese chose to leave and return to Portugal, and this process was accelerated in the months following independence. Today only a very small number of Portuguese still live in Angola, and nearly all of them can be found in the capital city.

A DISPLACED PEOPLE

The civil war spawned a disastrous humanitarian crisis in Angola, internally displacing 4.28 million people—one-third of Angola's population. The government spent $187 million settling internally displaced persons (IDPs) between April 4, 2002, and 2004. After that the World Bank gave $33 million to continue the settling process. The United Nations Office for the Coordination of Humanitarian Affairs (OCHA) estimated that fighting displaced 98,000 people between January 1, 2002 and February 28, 2002, alone. IDPs, who are often unacquainted with their surroundings, make up 75 percent of all land mine victims.

LIFESTYLE

Local women doing their washing in a village in Angola.

CHAPTER 7

INCE 1961, WHEN THE FIRST WAVE of rebellion against colonial rule resulted in violent repression by the Portuguese, most Angolans have been profoundly affected by decades of strife and civil war.

The United Nations has estimated the number of people killed in fighting at over half a million, with a similar number—mostly young children—dying from preventable diseases and malnutrition brought about by the civil war. Another 2 million people have lost their homes, and about 50,000 children have lost their parents.

It has been estimated that in just three years between 1993 and 1996 the number of refugees and migrants setting up home in the capital increased by 20 percent.

Women sell goods at a market in Luanda.

THE *MUSSEQUES*

The term *shantytown*—known as *musseque* ("MUS-seek") in Luanda—describes a poor part of town, where people live in crudely built shacks. The name comes from the characteristic red sand found in coastal Luanda that forms the floor of the makeshift compounds that make up a *musseque*. About 3 million people—most of whom were not born in the city—live in the shantytowns of Luanda. Families fled to the capital city from their village communities in fear for their lives during the war, and in the shanties where they now live they have a relative degree of safety.

A *musseque* is usually built around small compounds of about 270 square feet (25 square m) with up to six single-story houses inside. The compound itself is usually surrounded by a wall of corrugated iron sheets or concrete blocks.

Daily life is hard for these people living in the slums of Luanda.

LIFE IN A *MUSSEQUE*

The day begins at dawn. Often a woman starts the day's work by boiling water for coffee and breakfast. Clothes that have been left out to dry overnight need to be taken down and put away. The washing of clothes is a daily activity, and clean garments are folded and kept in plastic bags. Water is always needed and getting it often involves a trip on foot with buckets to the nearest standpipe. Even then the supply is irregular and cannot be relied on. Poor people are forced to buy water from private contractors at prices that can be as much as 10,000 times more than what people pay for piped water in the comfortable suburbs. The risks of this form of water supply, together with nonexistent sanitation and waste disposal, led to serious outbreaks of cholera in both 2006 and 2007. Some homes have access to a water tank that holds 1,400 gallons (5,000 liters) or more and can be refilled by a tanker. The family washes each morning, using cold water, no matter what time of year it is. In Luanda, winters are relatively mild, reaching a minimum temperature of 57°F (14°C).

People who see Luanda as their permanent home are more likely to take part in one of the many self-help projects designed to improve the quality of life. Establishing running water and a regular supply of electricity, the proper disposal of garbage, and the provision of public toilets are all major concerns. In rural areas limited access to safe water and sanitation has led the government to promise major investments in a "water for all" program that will aim to cover 80 percent of the population by 2012.

CITY LIFE

Many young people who travel to the nearest large town hoping to find employment and a better life are greatly disappointed. Life in a *musseque* is hard, and in Luanda, which attracts the majority of young people from the countryside, three-quarters of the population live in extreme poverty. Jobs are scarce, and there is always an urgent need to earn enough money to buy food. Obtaining fresh water is a constant problem. It has been estimated that the average family in the capital spends the equivalent of almost a day every week traveling to a source of fresh water, lining up for their turn, and then returning home. Poor families live on fish, because it is the cheapest food available.

Street children who have been left to fend for themselves are a common sight in Luanda. They survive by begging for food and a few coins, and they may be tempted to engage in illegal activities. In recent years crime in the cities has increased significantly. Desperate people have been driven to burglary, theft, and other more serious crimes.

Families collecting and storing clean water in Luanda.

Vehicles dot the busy streets of Luanda.

RURAL LIFE

In rural areas most Angolans live in village communities. The typical family is extended, with grandparents and other relatives living with the husband and wife and their children. Most children will only spend their younger years in the family home because the lure of the city is powerful, especially for young men. The city offers the possibility of employment and the chance to receive some form of education.

Angolans who live in the countryside depend on their farms for their livelihood. They may own some land, or a small group of families may rent a plot from the Ministry of Agriculture. The planting and harvesting of beans and cassava sustain many small farms. Toward the end of each year the fields are weeded and prepared for a new planting of crops. The December rainfall provides a good start for the new crop, as November to April is the start of the rainy season.

In many rural areas there are more women than men. This often results in families being headed by a woman, a significant change from traditional rural life, in which the male figure was the customary head of the family. But whether the woman is the head of the household or not, women usually do more work than men in the fields, looking after the crops and harvesting them.

Men are more likely to take charge of the family's cattle, following an age-old tradition across many parts of Africa. The average extended family may have a herd of about 20 cattle. Each year one or two of these cattle may be sold for cash to buy necessities that the family cannot grow or produce themselves.

Another way rural families may earn some extra cash is by working in traditional crafts, such as making household and kitchen items. There is always a demand for cooking utensils and farming tools, and many women earn a small but valuable income this way. For centuries women in African societies have been known for making pottery.

A village south of Luanda.

A market in Cuito, where Angolans sell their things to earn income to buy necessities.

THE MARKET

In Luanda and other towns the local market most families go to the market every day. A variety of produce is available, and it is in the market that essential foodstuffs are bought. In the countryside the local market may be a day's walk away, and villagers go to the market whenever they need to buy something or when they have some surplus food to sell.

Luanda's main market is the largest in the country and one of the largest in Africa. Every morning, shortly after dawn, more than 50,000 traders descend on the marketplace with their stock of food and other items for sale. They arrive in trucks and cars of all sizes, packed to the brim with produce. Because of the large number of traders in the market, a mini-economy devoted to feeding all those who work there every day has sprung up.

The Luanda market is far more than just a food market. It is the African equivalent of a huge shopping mall where everything that a family might need may be found. Even in the 1980s, when the government tried to outlaw private economic activity, the Luanda market continued to operate as a huge black market. For many of Luanda's poor, the market provides a living.

Angola's first-ever shopping mall opened in Luanda on December 14, 2008, with 100 stores, eight movie theaters, a restaurant area, banks, travel agents, attractions, and 900 parking spots. The huge consumer palace, made possible by foreign investors and a quickly growing Angolan middle class, shows that postwar Angola is gradually getting back to normal.

Despite their diffi-
cult circumstances,
Angolan children
still display a great
deal of dedication
in their makeshift
classrooms.

EDUCATION

During the Angolan civi war (1975—2002), nearly half of all schools were reportedly looted and destroyed, leading to current problems with overcrowding. The high dropout rate limited net enrollment to only 56 percent in 2005. In provinces hardest hit by the war, gross enrollment rates averaged less than 40 percent.

Teachers tend to be underpaid, inadequately trained, and overworked (sometimes teaching two or three shifts a day). Teachers also reportedly demand payment or brides directly from their students. Other factors, such as the presence of land mines, lack of resources and identity papers, and poor health, also prevent children from attending school regularly. Although education budgets were increased in 2004, the education system in Angola continues to be extremely underfunded. Still the Ministry of Education hired 20,000 new teachers in 2005 and continues to train teachers. Literacy is quite low, with only 67.4 percent of the population over the age of 15 able to read and write in Portuguese. As of 2001, 82.9 percent of males and 54.2 percent of women were literate.

Education for chil-
dren between the
ages of 7 and 15
is provided free by
the government.

Under Portuguese rule the Angolan people were classified as "natives" and were not allowed to enjoy the "benefits" of European civilization until they had undergone the process of assimilado, *or assimilation. To be assimilated means to be absorbed into a larger group, and in Angola this meant that an African had to abandon his or her traditional culture and adopt European customs and habits.*

Strict rules laid down the conditions: a minimum age of 18, fluency in the Portuguese language, a clean police record, and a job that paid a salary. Beyond these rules lay a clear understanding that an Angolan had to be prepared to turn his or her back on traditional village culture and adopt the manners and dress of the Portuguese. An Angolan had to apply to become an assimilado *and, if he or she was successful, a special identity card was issued to show that the holder had adopted a new cultural identity. The modern generation of Angolans no longer have to undergo this process.*

HEALTH

The low level of health care available and the poverty that affects most Angolans means that many children born in Angola never have a chance to grow up. For every 1,000 children born, about 260 will die before they reach the age of five.

In many other countries children are immunized against diseases that can prove fatal in their early years. In Angola only about one in three children receives injections to protect them against diseases such as measles and polio. Most parents do not know the value of simple vaccinations because they have never been informed about them. The lack of health-care centers, doctors, and trained nurses and midwives also means that for every mother who goes to a hospital to give birth, another mother will deliver at home without even the help or advice of a midwife. The maternal mortality rate in Angola is 2,800 per 100,000 pregnant women—one of the highest in the world—and less than 25 percent of births in 2003 were attended by a qualified health worker.

Opposite: A severely malnourished child has her weight monitored. Many Angolans suffer from abject poverty and the death toll from malnourishment is extremely high.

Medical personnel promote health care in Kuando Kubango.

Under colonial rule health care in Angola was left mainly to religious missions and, in the towns, to privately run clinics. After independence the government took over the responsibility of providing its citizens with basic health care but failed to allocate sufficient funds. With the outbreak of civil war health care received even less priority. Over 60 percent of primary health-care centers were destroyed in the civil war. There are few doctors and nurses in Angola. Many of them are non-Angolans working in Luanda, and they are often employed in private clinics, which few of the poor can afford. Although government-run clinics are available in Luanda, the lack of trained staff is a serious problem.

In rural areas people depend on clinics run by religious organizations. Many also still rely on traditional healers, who use spells and magical potions to rid the body of unhelpful spirits that are believed to be the cause of certain health problems. The 2006—2007 national report on HIV/AIDS in Angola shows the rate of HIV/AIDS infection to be only 2.1 percent of the population, which is considerably lower than in neighboring countries. One interesting explanation for this is that there is an unusually high percentage of circumcised men in Angola, which may lower the risk of infection.

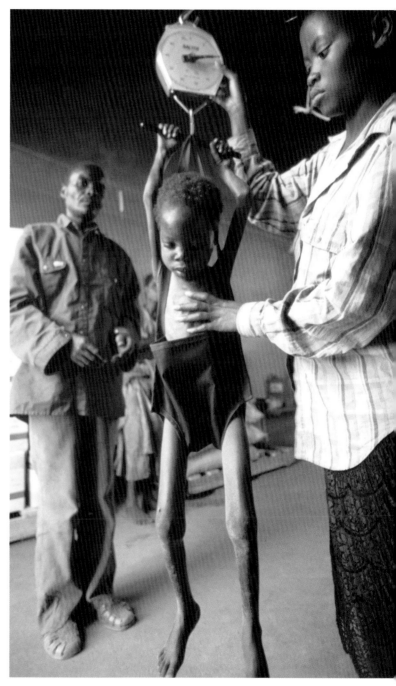

RELIGION

Pope Benedict XVI celebrates Mass at the San Paulo church in Luanda.

MANY ANGOLANS TEND TO FOLLOW customary beliefs and practices that are usually called traditional religions. This is a broad term that is used to describe African religious beliefs that are not part of Christianity or Islam. A large portion of the population also professes to be Christian, mainly Roman Catholic. Angola has virtually no Muslim population, which is unusual for an African nation.

Spiritual beliefs still play an important role in Angolan life today.

All religion was discouraged by the left-wing government in Luanda after independence was achieved in 1975. Religious institutions lost their schools, clinics, and properties. But when the MPLA abandoned communism, religious organizations regained influence, especially the Roman Catholic Church.

THE LIVING DEAD

The term *living dead* may sound like something from a horror movie, but it refers to the fundamental belief in Angola and other parts of Africa that the meaning of a person's life does not end with the death of his or her body. This belief is not the Christian idea of the resurrection of the soul or the notion that people will ultimately be judged according to their life on earth.

There is also no sense of heaven and hell in traditional religions in Angola. Even the idea of an all-powerful God—so central to both Islam and Christianity—is not linked to the tremendous reverence that a person may receive after death. When people die they may be remembered by name for 100 years or more, with their memory being passed down through three generations through word of mouth. A family shrine may even contain remnants of their bones to revere them and keep their memory alive.

In a sense the dead remain members of their families long after they have died. If misfortune befalls a family member, the family may consult an expert in these matters—a "diviner," sometimes also called a witch doctor—to find out if a deceased person is unhappy about something. In Angola the diviner is known as the *kimbanda* ("kim-BAN-da"). If the deceased is deemed to be unhappy, the *kimbanda* will perform a ritual to placate the spirit.

DIVINATION

In Angolan society, a diviner is someone who uses special means to find out something about the world of the supernatural. In larger villages the diviner is a specialist who usually works with his own divination basket. The basket

A religious symbol of the Chokwe people.

Fetish is a term from anthropology—the study of cultures—for describing an object that is worshiped by a people because of a belief in the object's magical or spiritual quality. The Kongo people who live in northern Angola and southern Democratic Republic of the Congo have fetish figures that are believed to be able to absorb—and, hence, render harmless—misfortunes brought about by evil spirits.

A person who feels he is the victim of an evil influence will stick nails in the fetish. Nail fetishes are made from wood for this special purpose. Sometimes the figure is created with a space inside where magical medicines can be stored. The medicine, often made from local plants, is not used for bodily illnesses, but to remove the evil spirit that has afflicted the sufferer.

contains a number of small ritual objects, such as clay figurines, pieces of polished metal, carved pieces of bone, and the teeth or horns of animals.

Special prayers are made to the ancestors of the clients, and the diviner shakes up the basket as part of the ritual. Then the diviner studies the arrangement of the objects once they have settled and gives his or her interpretation. Many diviners also have knowledge of herbal medicine.

Diviners are usually consulted when an individual has an illness or complaint of some kind that is thought to have a spiritual cause. The diviner hopes to identify the cause and fix the problem with the appropriate prayers. Some diviners specialize in certain illnesses. The more respected a diviner is, the larger the fee he or she is able to charge for his or her services.

CHRISTIANITY

Christianity began in Angola with the arrival of the Portuguese toward the end of the 15th century. Their first contact inland was with the Kongo kingdom, and there was a difference of opinion within the kingdom over the best way to deal with the European presence. The king at the time, Afonso Mvemba, a Nzinga, overcame his brother in a battle waged at Mbanza Kongo with the help of the Portuguese. He was an early convert to Roman Catholicism and

This Catholic church in Huambo is a legacy of Portugal, Angola's former colonial ruler.

changed his name to King Afonso I. He was the first African Christian to wield power in Angola, and through his influence the new religion spread with the help of Portuguese priests.

In the late 19th and early 20th centuries missionaries introduced Protestantism. Several Christian societies, including Protestant societies from North America, sent missionaries to Africa and they eventually reached Angola. Jonas Savimbi, the founder of UNITA, was a student at the school run by Canadian and U.S. Congregationalists. Initially the process of conversion was slow. For a long time missionary stations were confined to the coastal region. In the early 20th century, however, missionaries began to make an impact. A major reason for this was that a missionary station often offered some elementary education and basic health services. Over time these services attracted large numbers of people who had no other way of acquiring literacy or gaining access to health care.

Throughout the years of civil war Christian churches were never banned outright. However, the power of the Catholic Church diminished in the decade after independence, partly because the MPLA government did not want to encourage any organization that might rival its own power. Today Christian missions continue to operate in Angola.

Afonso's son Henrique was sent to Europe to be educated. Henrique became an ordained priest and returned to Kongo in the early 1520s to run Kongo's new church.

GOOD *The missionaries established the first schools in Angola for the non-Portuguese. They needed converts who would agree to become Christian teachers. In return they offered free education. They performed a valuable role in opening the door for black Angolans to educate themselves. Missions also established a rudimentary health service that benefited many people.*

BAD *The first missionaries in Angola actively supported the slave trade. They argued that they were saving the souls of the godless Africans. As late as 1870 a marble chair on the docks at Luanda was reserved for the bishop who baptized Angolans by the hundreds as they were rowed in chains on their way to the slave ships that would transport them across the Atlantic Ocean.*

The missionaries who first spread Christianity in Angola did not understand or respect traditional African forms of belief. They dismissed what they viewed as childish superstition and worked to replace it with their own beliefs and cultural values. Traditional African cultural practices were condemned by missionaries who did not understand their role within African society.

LANGUAGE

Students reading in a makeshift classroom in Angola.

>>T HE OFFICIAL NATIONAL language of Angola is Portuguese, and it is quickly becoming a national language rather than only an official language. A total of 80 percent of Angolans speak Portuguese, and for 60 percent of them, it is their main spoken language. Other Angolans are brought up as a member of a particular ethnic group and learn to speak the language of that group as well as Portuguese.

Pro-MPLA graffiti in Luanda.

Many people do not learn to read or write their non-Portuguese African language. Indeed, before European colonization spread across Africa, most cultures with their own languages did not have a written form. Europeans often mistook the absence of a written language as evidence of underdevelopment, failing to understand that a culture can have a sophisticated form of communication that can transmit information across generations without the need for a written form. In such cultures what is important is the oral tradition, and this is very true of Angolan society.

ORAL TRADITION

In the mid-1970s, during the civil war, one faction arrived in a village and tried to gain the support of the villagers. The following story was told as a way of communicating with the people:

One day there was a rabbit who wanted to marry the daughter of a bear. The rabbit went to the bear and asked for his permission, but the bear refused and told the rabbit that only someone who could build a house in

Angolans at a roadside stall. Angolan oral tradition includes many folk tales that feature slow-thinking bears and cunning, quick-witted rabbits.

Most Angolan students of all ages learn to read and write in Portuguese, the national language.

one day would be a suitable match for his beautiful daughter. The rabbit went away and gathered from his large family all the rabbits who looked like him. Then, making sure that the bear only ever saw one rabbit at any one time, they all worked together and succeeded in building a house in just one day. The bear, suitably impressed, gave permission to the clever rabbit to marry his daughter.

This story was readily understood by the villagers as a parable promoting the idea of working together for a common end. Angolans would have been taught through stories and fables from early childhood.

PORTUGUESE

Portuguese is the national language, and more people speak Portuguese in Angola than in any other African nation. In the towns and cities daily life is conducted in Portuguese. According to a census 99 percent of Luanda's population speaks Portuguese. Only in rural areas do people use their ethnic African language regularly.

Besides Portuguese, many Angolans also speak their tribal language.

FORÇA LÍDER NO DESENVOLVIMENTO DE ANGOLA

SONANGOL

A billboard advertising Angolan development in Luanda.

Portuguese is still widely spoken today because of historical reasons. It was the language of the ruling class who colonized the country, relegating the various ethnic languages of Angolans to an inferior role. The mother tongues of the ethnic groups were not acknowledged and were not used in any dealings between the colonial powers and the ordinary people. Any Angolan who wanted to receive an education and get a job outside of farming had little choice but to learn Portuguese.

The need for Angolans to learn Portuguese was an essential aspect of the *assimilado* process. A formal language test required an Angolan to show fluency in both speaking and writing Portuguese.

The Portuguese language spoken in Angola today is called "Angolan Portuguese," as it has been influenced by the several African languages spoken in Angolan, especially Kimbundu.

LANGUAGE GROUPS

Angolans have a strong sense of ethnic and regional identity. One main reason for this is because the different ethnic groups have their own languages. The Ovimbundu people, the largest group in the country, speak Umbundu—the language most commonly used and understood in central and southern Angola. Kimbundu, the language of the second-largest ethnic group, the Mbundu, is spoken mainly in the provinces of Luanda, Kwanza Norte, and Malanje.

Historically Luanda province is the area that has been most influenced by the Portuguese, and so, not surprisingly, the legacy of colonization on language has been most keenly felt by the Mbundu who live there. They generally speak Portuguese and, in many cases, the use of Angolan Portuguese is more prevalent than the native language.

Some African words, such as *maka* ("MAR-ka"), meaning "problem," and the local term for a diviner, *kimbanda*, have entered the Angolan Portuguese language.

In the northwest of Angola, in the provinces of Zaire and Uíge, the Kikongo language is spoken by the Bakongo people. This language is also spoken by people who belong to the same ethnic group in the neighboring countries of Congo and the Democratic Republic of the Congo. There are also some small subgroups of Bakongo people living in Cabinda who speak a dialect of Kikongo.

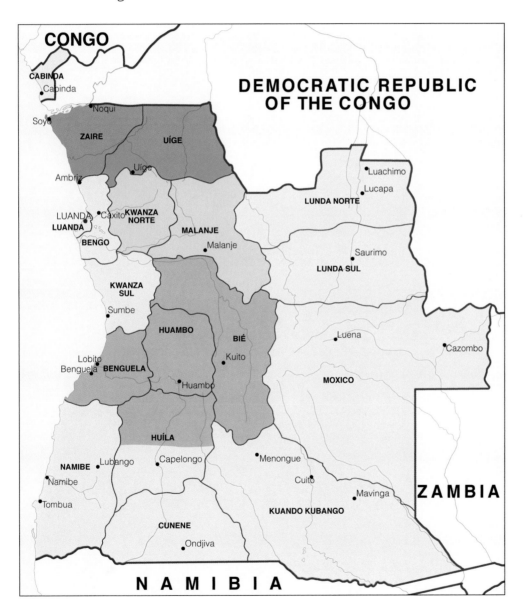

Main Languages Spoken in Angola

- Umbundu
- Kimbundu
- Kikongo

An Angolan vendor sells newspapers along the streets of Luanda.

UMBUNDU

In its traditional form, Umbundu, the language of the Ovimbundu, uses various proverbs and sayings that are rooted in the lives of the people who speak the language. Two examples are expressions that translate as "We have roots in the fields of our ancestors" and "The advocate speaks, the king decides." In an Umbundu conversation the speaker who uses one of these sayings will do so within a particular context, and usually the person being spoken to would interpret the remark in the light of that context.

For example, if there were a disagreement over who owned a plot of land and someone made the remark about roots in the fields of ancestors, this might be understood in terms of a claim to ownership based on a family relationship. If the other speaker replied by quoting the remark about advocates and kings, this might be understood as a way of saying that the matter needs to go to arbitration.

THE MEDIA

In Angola the government controls all media with nationwide reach, including radio, which is the most influential medium outside of the capital. Television, the private press, and Internet access are very limited outside of Luanda. There is one state-run national daily, the *Jornal de Angola*, and Luanda has several weekly newspapers. The official government newspaper is the *Diario da Republica*. Regional newspapers are also published in several towns.

The state-owned Rádio Nacional de Angola (RNA) broadcasts in Portuguese, English, French, Spanish, and several tribal languages, including Kimbundu, Umbundu, Kikongo, and Chokwe. Private stations operate in the main cities, including the Catholic station Radio Ecclesia, but RNA is the only available broadcaster across much of the country. In 2000 there were about 74 radios and 19 television sets for every 1,000 people. Pay TV services are operated by MultiChoice Angola and TV Cabo; they carry some Brazilian and Portuguese channels. The TV service TPA is state-owned and rarely criticizes the government.

Local men enjoying a sports show on television.

ARTS

An Angolan drummer performs in Luanda.

POPULAR TRADITIONAL ART FORMS in Angola include sculpture, mask-making, and music and dance. These flourish alongside everyday art forms such as pottery and basketwork. At the individual level Angolans express their artistic sense by creating beautiful hairstyles and headdresses that are usually decorated with a variety of colorful adornments. Angolans also have a tradition of scarification, designed to enhance the visual beauty of the body.

Artists put up their paintings at a park in Luanda.

SCULPTURE

Sculpture is one of Angola's oldest art forms. The earliest sculptures were done with wood and ivory, but modern sculptors also use metal as a base material. Originally the designs that inspired sculptors had their origins in traditional religious beliefs and were often abstract in form. The arrival of Europeans in the 16th century exposed Angolans to Christian imagery, and this has had an important influence on Angolan artists.

Another important influence that still plays a part in contemporary Angolan sculpture has been European and North American interest in ethnic African art. This has had the effect of introducing non-African pictorial ideas as subjects for sculptors. For instance, a traditional subject often portrayed by Angolan artists is that of the disgruntled ancestor who bewails the fact that he has not been shown the proper respect by his living ancestors. Small carved objects of such figures are familiar items in the diviner's basket of ritual objects.

A throne sculpture from Angola's past.

Sazangwiyo, a Chokwe artist who is familiar with French sculptor Auguste Rodin's statue of *The Thinker*, used the disgruntled ancestor figure to produce a modern African version of Rodin's famous image. Sazangwiyo's sculpture has since become well known and is often imitated.

MASK PAINTING

Mask painting brings together the art of sculpture and the art of painting. The mask itself is usually made of wood or by using a wicker frame and lining it with bark cloth. The cloth or wooden surface is then painted. Masks are used in rituals and ceremonies, such as those to mark the transition from childhood to adulthood and the celebration of a new harvest.

The start of the hunting season may also be marked by a mask ceremony, with some masks painted to represent the animals that the community hopes to hunt successfully.

CHOKWE ART

Chokwe art is renowned for the quality of its wooden sculptures. The best examples were made between the 16th and mid-19th centuries, when the Chokwe were under Lunda rule. After 1860 the Chokwe rose up against the Lunda and even dominated them, but the sculpture of this period is not considered as good.

A feature common to Chokwe art is the large upturned hairstyles on figures, possibly a reflection of what was once a fashion among the leading chiefs and their families. Chokwe sculptures often portray their leaders with hands and feet on a clearly exaggerated scale—a pair of hands, for example, would be significantly larger than the figure's head. This signifies the great power and strength of the rulers.

The Chokwe people are also known for the quality of their weapons, some of which bear the fine decorative motifs used by woodcarvers.

The Mbwela people
have two kinds of
masked figures.
The masks worn by
men are known as
the *makisi avamala*
("ma-KI-si a-va-
MAR-la"), while the
masks of women
are called the
makisi avampwevo
("ma-KI-si a-vam-
PWEV-o"). In reality
the women do not
wear masks that
cover their heads,
but instead color
their bodies with
paint and only
cover their hair.

ANGOLAN PAINTERS

In the second half of the 20th century a number of Angolan artists achieved international recognition for their paintings. One of the earliest and most famous is José zan Andrade, more familiarly known as Zan. He was born in 1946 and taught himself how to paint. He first became known for his work in Chinese ink painting and gouache, a method of painting that uses opaque pigments ground in water and mixed with a glue-like substance. Contemporaries of Zan, who have been influenced more by modern art movements, include Tomas Vista (born in 1957) and Paulo Jazz (born 1940).

WEAVING

The art of weaving first developed as a practical skill, mainly to produce mats for use in the home. When imported machine-made textiles became more readily available, the art of weaving in Angola went into decline. Only recently, beginning in the 1980s, have Angolan women revitalized the art. Today weaving has emerged as a specialized art that caters to an international market, although weavers still draw on traditional motifs for their designs

Baskets from Huíla province woven from reeds.

and ideas. One of the most successful contemporary weavers is Maria Luiza da Silva, who first learned the skill of weaving from her family before going on to study the subject at art school. She works with wool and burlap, creating subtle and complex designs on tapestries.

SONG AND DANCE

Song, dance, and music are all fundamental aspects of traditional African culture. Regions that are widely separated geographically may have surprisingly similar forms of song and dance, and although no one has been able to explain these similarities, they can presumably be traced back to an earlier time when these art forms were first being developed. For example, in parts of eastern Angola, there is a form of multipart singing that uses exactly the same tone as that found among an ethnic group in Côte d'Ivoire in West Africa.

An all-male group sings and plays guitars.

Nevertheless some forms of Angolan dance are unique to the country. In the southwest of Angola, for example, the Nkili dance uses a pair of dancers to very dramatic effect. At the climax of the dance the male dancer leaps into the air, landing with his hands on the shoulders of the female dancer, who balances him on her shoulders. Such a dance requires constant practice and strong shoulders on the part of the woman.

One attempt to understand and classify the great variety of African dance styles is based on the idea that different styles use different parts of the body. European dance, by comparison, is said to treat the body as a single whole. According to this system, many of the Angolan dance forms revolve around the movement of the pelvis to create a characteristic form.

Another type of Angolan dance is characterized by the use of masked dancers, who use a greater variety of movements. Each set of movements, using a particular part of the body, has its own name in the local language.

A group of traditional dancers.

MASKED DANCES

Dances based on the use of masks are fairly unique to west and west-central Africa. The region bounded by eastern Angola and parts of Zambia and the Democratic Republic of the Congo is one of the richest sources of masked dancing on the continent. There is a wide variety of masks, and each ethnic group has its own colors and designs. Just as important is the function or meaning attached to a particular mask, because this helps convey the story behind the mask or the significance associated with a specific mask.

Many Angolan masks represent ancestral members of a prestigious royal family. Some masks represent officials and servants of the court. Masked dances thus perform a function similar to that of oral tradition—they help preserve a sense of history and identity that is not dependent on books and writing. When performing a dance the person wearing the mask also uses gestures and pantomime-like actions to convey the character represented by the mask.

Masked dancers in Huíla province.

DANCE OF THE NDZINGI

The Mbwela people celebrate in mask form the character of the ndzingi, *a figure from Angolan folklore who lives far away from people in the forest. He is a giant, and this is depicted by a grand mask with a huge head that is built up from a frame of wood that is then covered with barkcloth.*

Ndzingi usually appears as a menacing figure that stomps and rages while threatening the audience with a bundle of twigs that he waves around him. Suddenly, and very dramatically, his behavior changes to represent a figure who seems drunk, trying to hold himself together before finally collapsing in a heap on the ground. The audience laughs in relief at the spectacle of a giant whose head was too heavy for his own body.

MUSICAL INSTRUMENTS

Angolan music is produced using a rich variety of traditional musical instruments. A typical example of a percussion instrument is the *saxi* ("SAR-ki"), more commonly known as maracas. In Angola these are made from the dried fruit known as *maboque* ("MA-boo-ker") and are filled with dried seeds or glass beads.

Drums, known as bongos or tam-tam, vary in size from one region to another, but they are often a popular instrument for accompanying dancing. In the past drums were used to send messages. Other traditional instruments include the marimba, a type of xylophone, and the *xingufos* ("SING-U-fos"), which are large antelope horns that have been cleaned and dried.

A rare Angolan instrument is the *sagaya* ("sar-GA-ya") of the Humbi people in the southwest of the country. An ordinary hunting bow is fitted with

Agostinho Neto, the first president of independent Angola, was widely recognized as an accomplished poet. Born in 1922 in Bengo province, Neto studied medicine in Lisbon. He first became known at the age of 26 when he published a volume of poems and joined a national cultural movement aimed at rediscovering indigenous Angolan culture. Neto died in Moscow in 1979. The following lines are taken from one of Neto's poems, "Fire and Rhythm":

> *Rhythm in light*
> *rhythm in color*
> *rhythm in movement*
> *rhythm in the bloody cracks of bare feet*
> *rhythm on torn nails*
> *Yet rhythm*
> *rhythm.*

> *Oh painful African voices.*

a mouth brace, and the player breathes through the brace while stroking the bow's string with a fine twig-like strip of leather. As the player changes his breathing and the position of his mouth, the tone produced by playing the string changes.

Another, more common string instrument is the *hungu* ("HUNG-go"). A small stick, held in the right hand, plays the bow, which is held at stomach level. The hungu was taken to Brazil in the days of slavery, and it is now known in South America as the *berimbau* ("bur-IM-ba").

Opposite: A young Angolan playing the *berimbau.*

Arts **109**

LEISURE

Mosaics and rainbow-colored café umbrellas
decorate a city sidewalk in Benguela.

CHAPTER 11

DEVASTATED BY DECADES OF CIVIL war, the people of Angola have had less opportunity to enjoy leisure time than people in many other parts of the world. Today, as in the past, the family provides an emotional foundation for the enjoyment of leisure time. Leisure for many people is the informal social life of the home and the village community.

The years of civil war disrupted family life and forced many people to rely on themselves. The massive drift of population to Luanda and other urban centers has also caused overcrowding, widespread unemployment, and a general sense of insecurity.

Still a determination to survive has characterized life in these difficult circumstances. Most families have been divided or traumatized by the war, but Angolans have managed to find times to come together and enjoy one another's company. This is part of the rebuilding of Angola.

Angolan men enjoying a game of foosball.

A DAY AT THE BEACH

Luanda has a beautiful, natural bay with a sandy beach. This bay was where the Portuguese first landed and where, in the centuries that followed, thousands of poor Portuguese arrived to start a new life in Africa. Today the same beach is open to everyone and provides relaxation and recreation for the poor people of the city. On the weekend especially, the beach is crowded with families.

On one side of the bay is a narrow peninsula of land that stretches into the sea. On the weekends both sides of this peninsula are crowded with Angolans enjoying picnic lunches. During the week people also come to the beach to relax after work and to escape from the drudgery of shantytown life. Mussulo Island nearby attracts weekend visitors who are able to organize the boat ride there and back.

Apart from enjoying a sunny day out at the beach, Angolans often take part in a game of beach volleyball.

A *MUSSEQUE* EVENING

During the week leisure time in a Luanda shantytown revolves around the evening meal. With family members leaving for work at different times, the evening meal is an occasion for everyone to come together and talk about their day. The father may have some good news, even if it is only a rumor that new water pipes are going to be laid down or that the electricity station that used to provide power to the *musseque* is finally being repaired. The mother may announce that she has sold more than the usual amount of food at the market that day. After the meal oil lanterns and perhaps a fire in the yard outside will be lit. The family may gather around and continue their conversation.

Before going to bed, some chores may be completed—water may need to be collected for the morning, or wet clothes may need to be hung out to dry.

LEISURE IN THE COUNTRYSIDE

A traditional form of leisure in the countryside is for a small group of friends or neighbors to gather and talk around an open fire, especially when a full moon provides plenty of light. An interesting or amusing story, perhaps first brought to the village by someone who has been working in Luanda, will be told more than once. A more traditional story may be told by one of the respected elders of the village. Sometimes such a story is accompanied by someone playing a marimba drum, made by attaching a sheet of bamboo or metal to a board that acts as a resonator. The board is held in both hands and played with the thumbs.

Some rural areas are visited regularly by a traveling movie group that brings its own equipment and movies. If there is no movie theater in the town and a suitable blank wall is not available to show the movie on, a large white sheet is hung over a wall as a substitute.

On the weekends dances are held regularly in the rural areas, perhaps accompanied by a live drum band. Smaller parties are held at home for special occasions, such as the birth of a child, and a radio broadcast provides music for dancing.

This is a folktale of the Mbangala people of Angola that goes back centuries to the time when the Lunda kingdom was first established by people from another kingdom—the Luba—in what is now the southeastern part of the Democratic Republic of Congo.

A young prince named Chibinda Ilunga came to the Lunda kingdom because he had an argument with the Luba king, who had accused Chibinda of being afraid to fight in war. The truth was that the Luba king was secretly jealous of Chibinda's great skill as a hunter. The queen of the Lunda people, named Lueji, was down by the riverside one morning when she met Chibinda for the first time. She was struck by his great beauty and natural manners. Before the day was over they had fallen in love.

In time they married, and in due course, Lueji announced to her court that Chibinda was now their king. He made a speech to the court and promised that as a hunter he would continue to kill animals, but that he would never shed the blood of another human being. This was accepted, but a problem arose when Lueji was unable to bear children. The difficulty was solved when Lueji found another woman, named Kamonga, who also became Chibinda's wife and bore him children.

SPORTS

Sports are very popular in Angola. The sports that attract the most participants and spectators are soccer, basketball, handball, swimming, and roller hockey. The Angola basketball team has won eight Federation of International Basketball (FIBA) Africa Championships, the first in 1989 and the most recent in 2007. They also won the basketball tournament for at the 2007 All-Africa Games. In track and field Angola has also enjoyed success. Jose Armando Sayovo was the first person to win a Paralympics medal for Angola, at the 2004 Summer Paralympics Games in Athens, when he won three gold medals, in the 100-, 200-, and 400-meter sprints.

CHESS CHAMPIONS

A successful tradition of competing in international chess competitions began in 1987 when, at age 17, Manuel Mateus became the youngest African player to gain the international status of chess master. Today Angola has 16 chess players who are ranked as international masters, and chess is a popular extracurricular activity in high schools.

Soccer is very popular, in part because it only requires one ball for 22 people to enjoy a game. Angola has a professional soccer league, but the best players are lured away to Portugal because of the higher wages players can earn there. Still Angola's national soccer team reached the finals in the 2006 World Cup, despite being ranked 78th in world soccer. In large towns it is not unusual for 75,000 spectators to fill the stadiums if one of the top soccer clubs is playing. Angolan women have also achieved notable success in sports. The Angolan women's team won the African championship in handball in 2008 while hosting the tournament.

Teenage boys playing soccer in Luanda.

FESTIVALS

A local Angolan participates in Carnival in Luanda.

PEOPLE IN ANGOLA ARE MORE LIKELY to remember festivals of the past than take part in contemporary ones. Traditional Angolan society celebrated major events in a person's life. The birth of a child, moving from adolescence to adulthood, and marriage were all viewed as important and were celebrated as festive occasions.

Local Angolan dancers perform during Carnival in Luanda.

It is not that festivals are no longer celebrated in Angola, only that many people today find it difficult to afford the food and drink that traditionally characterized a festival. The fracturing and separation of so many families because of the war has also made it more difficult for family members to get together for festive occasions. There is good reason to hope that in time the traditional exuberance that marked celebrations will once again become a lively aspect of Angolan society.

FAMILY FESTIVALS

In Angola communities enjoy the often impromptu social festivals that take place for occasions such as the birth of a child. The birth of a child is always a cause for celebration, and even among poor families, the occasion is marked in some way. A special meal is usually cooked at the earliest opportunity, often for the evening of the day when the child is born. Even if the mother travels to a clinic for the actual birth, she usually comes back home the same day.

A baby is christened by a Catholic priest.

A chicken or a duck is often considered a necessary part of the special meal. Sometimes a family member may give a gift of one of their chickens or ducks, and it will be killed and prepared within an hour. Neighbors will almost certainly pay a visit to wish the newborn a prosperous and happy future, and a small amount of money will be given as a gift for the child. The home needs to be cleaned up and made as presentable as possible for the visitors. If there is money for beer a few bottles are bought and offered to guests.

The baptism of a child, a Christian ceremony marking a spiritual stage in a child's life, is often followed by a small private celebration for family and neighbors. Parents and neighbors may also celebrate the first birthday of a child. When a daughter reaches the age of 18, her parents may present her to the community in a "coming out" party. In a small village this celebration might include nearly all of the villagers, although in a town the party would only be attended by family, friends, and neighbors.

An Angolan girl dances as youths await Pope Benedict XVI's arrival in Luanda.

CHRISTMAS AND EASTER

Christmas Day is usually celebrated in Angola with a special meal. Families try to gather as many members of the family as possible for the meal. They also try to save for the Christmas meal to be able to afford something special, such as swordfish, instead of a less expensive type of fish. Christians celebrate Christmas for its religious significance because the day is traditionally regarded as the birthday of Jesus Christ. Even non-Christians are likely to regard the day as a time for general goodwill and merriment. For the average Angolan, Christmas is more of a family occasion than a religious event.

Easter, which celebrates the belief that Christ was resurrected after his crucifixion, is the most important festival for Roman Catholics. Easter Sunday takes place between late March and early April, depending on the date of the first full moon after the spring equinox. The weeks before Easter are known as Lent, and they are traditionally observed as a period of abstinence to commemorate Christ's 40-day fast in the wilderness. In Angola this tradition of abstinence is reflected in the practice of not eating meat during Lent.

MARRIAGE

In the countryside it is not uncommon for Angolan parents to suggest a possible partner for their son or daughter. In some rural areas this goes

A bride on her wedding day.

With 2.1 billion Christians around the world, Christmas and Easter are among the world's most widely observed celebrations.

The following are the public holidays celebrated in Angola:

New Year's Day	January 1
Martyrs of the Colonial Repression Day	January 4
Luanda's Day	January 25
Start of Liberation War	February 4
International Women's Day	March 8
Peace and Reconciliation Day	April 4
Good Friday	Variable
Easter Monday	Variable
Labor Day	May 1
Africa Day	May 25
International Children's Day	June 1
Nation's Founder and National Heroes Day	September 17
All Saints' Day	November 1
All Souls' Day	November 2
Independence Day	November 11
Christmas Day	December 25

a step further, with arranged marriages still taking place regularly. However, in urban areas this practice is in decline, and it is more common for parents to simply pass on to their daughter a compliment that a man may have made about her. Such a compliment is made on the understanding that this might be interpreted as the first stage in a proposal of marriage.

Marriage is always a cause for celebration. Once the compulsory registration in a government office has taken place, there may be a church ceremony in which the bride wears white and the groom dresses up in a suit and tie. In practice many young couples will not be able to afford a white dress or a suit. But this will not keep them from celebrating. A special meal will be prepared, drinks will be available, and a party atmosphere will turn the event into a festive occasion. Singing and dancing always accompany the party.

Opposite: A Baluba man performs the Thief's Dance wearing pelts and bells.

CIRCUMCISION

The masked figure of the *ndzingi* is one of the most popular figures at circumcision festivals among the Mbwela people. The *ndzingi* first instills fear because of his frightful appearance, characterized by his large red-colored mouth, but this fear turns to laughter when he falls to the ground because his head is too large for his body.

Young boys in the audience run up and help him stand upright—but he soon collapses again. The combination of feelings evoked by the dance—first fear and then the relief of laughter—matches the emotions of many boys who take part in the circumcision ceremony.

High-spirited Carnival celebrations in Menongue.

FUNERALS

A funeral, known as a komba *("KUM-ba") in Angola, is not always as somber an affair as it is in the West. In traditional rural areas it is believed that the deceased will be happy if everyone celebrates. The* komba *is organized by close relatives and friends, and together, they cover the cost of the food and drink that is served to those who attend the funeral. Often the close friends are neighbors of the deceased, because in Angolan villages neighbors can become very close and may be regarded almost as part of the family.*

CARNIVAL

Carnival is the most popular festival in Angola. It is used to be celebrated at the end of March each year, marking the anniversary of the expulsion of invading South African troops. Carnival has now been moved to February. In Luanda, Carnival is celebrated on the streets with processions. The colorful and elaborately decorated floats that make up the main procession are the most striking aspect of the festivities.

A prize is awarded for the most impressive float, and various groups spend a lot of time designing and decorating their floats hoping to win the prize. Carnival is so popular in Luanda that troupes drive to the capital from rural areas in trucks, bringing their floats fully or partly made. When the main procession through the streets is over, the Carnival spirit continues until late in the night.

FOOD

A child sells homemade bread in a market.

FOR MOST ANGOLANS FINDING FOOD is at the heart of the struggle for survival. The idea of dining as a form of entertainment or being able to make choices about what to eat is rare for most people in Angola. A typical poor family usually does not eat meat because it cannot afford to do so. Only for special occasions will a family-owned chicken or duck be killed and cooked.

Young toddlers feeding on milk in Malange.

The residents of Luanda and other large towns depend on imported food, but the rest of the population, living in the countryside, lives off what they can grow, plus whatever small income they might make from selling surplus food.

SURVIVAL TACTICS

Corn is a crop that provides a rich source of starch as well as protein. However, growing corn requires regular weeding and a degree of care on the part of the farmer. Angolans have responded to war conditions by using land that was traditionally reserved for corn to grow millet, cassava, sweet potatoes, and sorghum.

Millet, for example, is also a grain grass, but it grows faster than corn and needs less weeding. Sorghum is far more resistant to drought than corn, so it requires less watering. People have also survived by taking any opportunity they get to fish in streams or lagoons. In the past this was regarded as a

Children selling various food products at a market in Angola.

secondary activity for women, but it is now practiced by all members of the family.

In Luanda and other large towns a limited form of agriculture has developed amid the tin shacks and concrete buildings. Pigs are a familiar sight in Luanda, and children are often used to keep a watchful eye on this valuable source of food. Wherever possible a family keeps a few chickens or goats, and the care of these animals often falls to the women and children.

CASSAVA

Cassava is the most important food crop in Angola. It can be made into a variety of foods—cassava flour, bread, tapioca—and even a laundry starch. An alcoholic brew can also be made from cassava. The raw root of the cassava is poisonous—it contains a cyanide-based sugar—and must be prepared carefully before it is safe to be eaten.

Traditionally the cassava root is processed by women. The first stage involves soaking the root and letting it dry completely. It is then pounded into flour using a mortar and pestle. Before the root is harvested the leaves of the plant can be removed and used to make *kizaka* ("kiz-AH-ka"), an Angolan dish made from vegetables. Another popular and inexpensive meal based on cassava is *fuba* ("FOO-bar"). Untreated cassava, known as *bombom* ("BOMB-bomb"), can be bought in towns by the bucketful.

A local woman balances fruits on her head at a market.

MEALS OF THE DAY

Breakfast usually consists of bread or *funje* ("PHON-jee"), a porridge made from cassava. Coffee is a popular drink. Although good-quality coffee is cultivated in Angola, most people drink instant coffee imported from abroad, because it is easier to get than the superior local coffee. Young children may be fed milk made from imported milk powder. Poorer families drink plain water.

Lunch is often quick and informal, especially for those who work, and may consist of bread with some cheese. The evening meal, on the other hand, is an occasion for most of the family to be together. It is often delayed until everyone has returned home.

Because few people can afford meat, vegetables and fish are more commonly eaten. In the towns meals and hot drinks are prepared using a stove fueled with bottled gas. Many homes in urban areas do not have a separate kitchen; the stove is found in the living room.

Some families also have a space outside their home for a small open fire, built using wood and charcoal, which saves the expense of bottled gas. Some people earn their living by collecting firewood in the countryside and then selling it in towns. A small supply of paraffin is usually kept to sprinkle over the wood to make it easier to light. In the countryside stoves are usually fueled by charcoal or coal, and the cooking often takes place outside the home in the open.

Grilled fish are easy to prepare and are popular in Angola.

Because Angola was a colony of Portugal for many years, the Portuguese influence upon Angolan cuisine was subtle but pervasive, bringing the European sense of flavoring with spices and techniques of roasting and marinating to traditional Angolan foods. These influences blended with the local cuisine and produced interesting new recipes. There are some differences between the ingredients used in the cuisine of the coast of Angola and those used in European cuisine. However, Angola is a large country with many regional flavors and ethnic cultures, but one of the elements these different regions have in common is the fact that Angolans like their food spicy. Angolan cuisine is varied and tasty, with local dishes based mainly on fish, cassava products, and spicy stews. The cuisine of Angola can be called a "rainbow cuisine" because it has integrated influences from India, Malaysia, and Europe. The food is a blend of many cultures in most regions of Angola.

LIVING BY BREAD ALONE

In Luanda one seldom needs to walk far before finding a bakery. Bread forms the basis of a quick lunch for many working people. Some people bake bread in their own homes and sell it by the roadside or in a market.

One bag of flour makes around 500 rolls, and a baker needs to know how many fresh rolls he hopes to sell before baking a new day's supply. In smaller towns and in the countryside a popular type of bread is *pao burro* ("pow BORE-o;" donkey's bread), which can be baked inexpensively at home in a simple wood-burning oven.

THE COST OF FOOD

The prices of basic foods have increased rapidly from 2007 to 2009. Due to climate change, the main grain-producing area in Angola has been hit continuously by both drought and flood. A large proportion of the family income goes to buy food.

Fuel is also needed to cook food. The cheapest fuels are firewood and charcoal, and the prices of these gradually increase as it becomes necessary to travel farther away from the city center to find a suitable supply.

KIZAKA PEANUT STEW

1 teaspoon (5 ml) vegetable oil

1 onion, diced

1 pound (450 g) collard greens, kale or spinach

$^3/_4$ cup (180 ml) toasted sesame seeds OR unsalted peanuts OR peanut butter

vegetable broth (optional)

3 tomatoes, chopped

salt and pepper, to taste

red pepper flakes, to taste

minced garlic to taste

minced ginger to taste

- In a large saucepan, cook the greens in boiling water until tender and drain. Vegetable broth may be added for flavor. Set aside.

- In a frying pan, sauté the onions in oil for 3 to 4 minutes before adding the garlic.

- Add the garlic and ginger and sauté until soft and aromatic.

- Add tomatoes and cook until tender.

- Then add sesame seeds/unsalted peanuts/ peanut butter. Continue cooking for about 5 minutes.

- Add greens to the mixture and season with salt, pepper, and pepper flakes. Cook together for a few minutes. Serve with hot rice.

YELLOW COCONUT PUDDING

2 cups (500 ml) sugar

4 whole cloves

12 egg yolks

6 cups (1.5 L) water

4 cups (400 g) grated coconut

ground cinnamon

- Combine half of the sugar, the cloves, and the water in a saucepan. Bring to a boil.

- Reduce heat to low. Take out the cloves and add the coconut.

- Mix thoroughly and cook 10 minutes over low heat. Remove from heat.

- Place the egg yolks in a deep bowl. Beat them with an electric mixer for 1 minute.

- Stir in the remaining sugar and the coconut mixture. Pour the mixture into the saucepan.

- Cook over medium heat for 10 minutes.

- Pour into individual dessert dishes or in a dessert tray. Sprinkle with cinnamon and refrigerate for 2 hours.

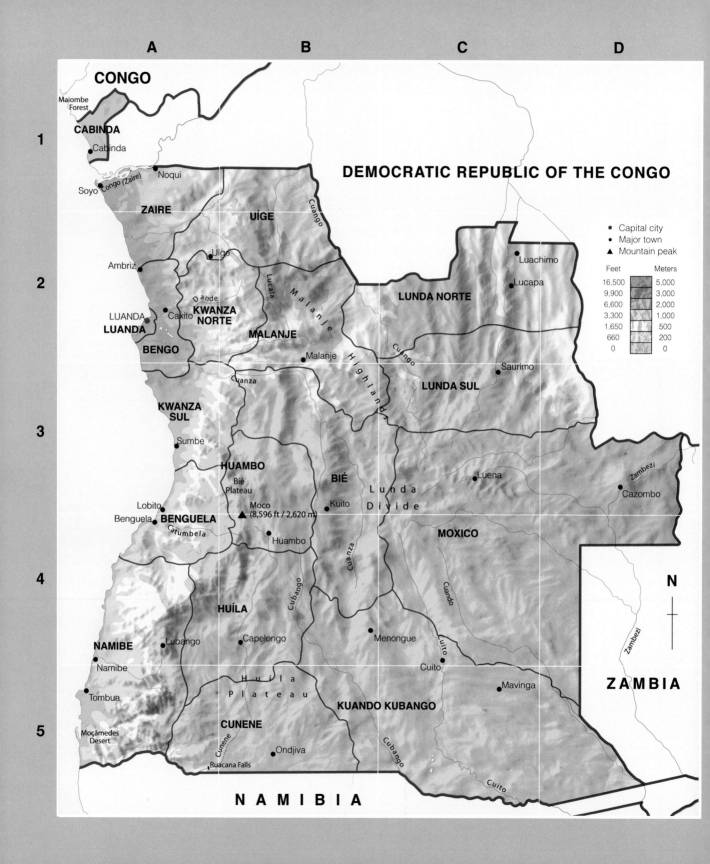

A **B** **C** **D**

1

CONGO

Maiombe
Forest

CABINDA

Cabinda

Noqui

Soyo Congo (Zaire)

ZAIRE

DEMOCRATIC REPUBLIC OF THE CONGO

UÍGE

Cuango

Uíge

Ambriz

Lucala

2

Malanje

Luachimo

Lucapa

LUNDA NORTE

• Capital city
• Major town
▲ Mountain peak

Feet   Meters
16,500   5,000
9,900   3,000
6,600   2,000
3,300   1,000
1,650   500
660   200
0   0

D ande

**KWANZA
NORTE**

LUANDA Cakito

LUANDA

BENGO

MALANJE

Malanje

Highlands

Cuango

Saurimo

LUNDA SUL

Cuanza

**KWANZA
SUL**

3

Sumbe

HUAMBO

Bié
Plateau

BIÉ

Kuito

Luena

Lunda

Cazombo

Zambezi

Lobito

Benguela **BENGUELA**

Catumbela

Moco
(8,596 ft / 2,620 m)

Huambo

Cu a n z a

Divide

MOXICO

4

Cubango

HUÍLA

Cuando

N

Lubango

Capelongo

Menongue

Cuito

Zambezi

NAMIBE

Namibe

H u í l a
P l a t e a u

Cuito

Mavinga

ZAMBIA

Tombua

5

Moçâmedes
Desert

CUNENE

Cunene

Ondjiva

Cubango

Ruacana Falls

Cuito

KUANDO KUBANGO

N A M I B I A

MAP OF ANGOLA

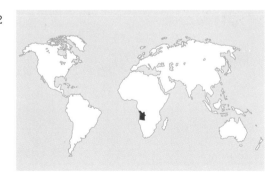

ECONOMIC ANGOLA

Agriculture

 Bananas

 Sugarcane

 Coffee

 Corn

 Tobacco,

 Sisal

 Cotton

Natural Resources

 Copper

 Diamonds

 Gold

 Granite

 Hydroelectricity

 Iron

 Petroleum

 Phosphate

 Quartz

 Uranium

Services

 Airports

 Tourism

 Ports

ABOUT THE ECONOMY

OVERVIEW

Angola's high growth rate is driven by its oil sector, which contributes to 85 percent of GDP. Increased oil production supported growth averaging more than 15 percent per year from 2004 to 2007. A postwar reconstruction boom and resettlement of displaced persons has also led to high growth rates in construction and agriculture. Much of the country's infrastructure is still damaged or undeveloped due to the 27-year-long civil war, and remnants of the conflict, such as widespread land mines, still mar the countryside. Subsistence agriculture provides the main livelihood for most of the people, but half of the country's food must still be imported. In 2005 the government started using a $2 billion line of credit, since increased to $7 billion, from China to rebuild Angola's public infrastructure, and several large-scale projects were completed in 2006.

GROSS DOMESTIC PRODUCT (GDP)

U.S.$95.95 billion (2008 estimate)

GDP GROWTH

15.1 percent (2008 estimate)

CURRENCY

Kwanza
1 kwanza=100 cêntimos
U.S.$1 = 75.1 kwanzas (March 2009)

WORKFORCE

7.29 million (2008 estimate)

UNEMPLOYMENT RATE

40 percent (2008 estimate)

INFLATION

12.5 percent (2008 estimate)

EXTERNAL DEBT

$7.9 billion (December 31, 2008, estimate)

MAJOR EXPORTS

Crude oil, diamonds, refined petroleum products, gas, coffee, sisal, fish and fish products, timber, cotton

MAJOR IMPORTS

Machinery and electrical equipment, vehicles and spare parts, medicines, food, textiles, military goods

MAIN TRADE PARTNERS

United States, China, France, Taiwan, South Africa, Portugal, Brazil, United Kingdom, Germany

NATURAL RESOURCES

Petroleum, diamonds, iron ore, phosphates, copper, feldspar, gold, bauxite, uranium

AGRICULTURAL PRODUCTS

Bananas, sugarcane, coffee, sisal, corn, cotton, manioc (tapioca), tobacco, vegetables, plantains, livestock, forest products, fish

CULTURAL ANGOLA

M'banza-Kongo
M'banza-Kongo is the capital of Zaire province. It sits on top of an impressive flat-topped mountain and is also known for the ruins of its 16th-century cathedral, which many Angolans claim is the oldest church in sub-Saharan Africa.

Luanda
Luanda, the capital of Angola, retains its heritage as a Portuguese colonial city, and there are several buildings of historical significance, such as the Museum of Armed Forces. Luanda is also adjacent to a beautiful bay.

Mussulo Island
Mussulo Island is an extension of land located in the south of Luanda and famous for its natural beauty. One can try aquatic sports and sample some of the local food, or simply relax under the numerous palm trees.

Parque Nacional da Kissama
Kissama is Angola's most accessible and well-stocked wildlife park. This huge swath of coastal savannah punctuated by gnarly baobab trees is home to elephants, water buffalo, indigenous palanca antelopes, and a precarious population of nesting sea turtles.

Benguela-Lobito Railway
Rattling and bumping through Benguela's rural hodgepodge is a unique and unforgettable Angolan experience. The railway line roughly follows old trade routes between the ancient trading center of Benguela and its hinterland of the Bië plateau.

Maiombe Rain Forest
The Maiombe rain forest is described by locals as "the vegetable sea" due to its canopy of luxuriant green vegetation. The forest covers an enormous area and is often described as "the Amazon of Africa." It is famous for its butterflies.

Calandula Falls
Located in the large central Angolan province of Malanje, the Calandula Falls in the Lucala River tumbles more than 328 feet (100 m) down and is Africa's second-largest waterfall after Victoria Falls. The falls' great width makes it a breathtaking sight.

Namibe
This province is the land of the *tumboa* (*Welwitschia mirabilis*), a carnivorous desert plant that resembles a giant octopus. The Namib Desert offers excellent hunting, and Namibe is one of the main fishing centers in Angola.

Lubango
Lubango is the capital of the province of Huíla. It is surrounded by mountains, and one of them has a statue of Jesus Christ with a fantastic view of the city. Lubango also provides access to the beautiful beaches of Namibe.

Iona National Park
Iona National Park is the largest park in the country. Illegal poaching and the destruction of infrastructure have caused considerable damage to the once rich park. The park is also known for unique flora and incredible rock formations.

Cameia National Park
There is flora and fauna in Cameia National Park that cannot be found anywhere else in Angola. Two lakes lie outside the park boundaries, and both have extensive reed beds and grassy swamps that are rich in aquatic birds.

ABOUT THE CULTURE

OFFICIAL NAME
Republic of Angola

CAPITAL
Luanda

POPULATION
12.8 million (2009 estimate)

MAIN CITIES
Sana'a, Aden, Ta'izz, Hodeida

OFFICIAL LANGUAGE
Portuguese (official), Bantu and other African languages

AREA
481,354 square miles (1,246,700 square kilometers)

NATIONAL FLAG
Two equal horizontal stripes of red and black, with a five-pointed star, half a cogwheel, and a machete superimposed in the center in gold

HIGHEST POINT
Mount Moco (8,596 feet/2,620 m)

ETHNIC GROUPS
Ovimbundu 37 percent, Kimbundu 25 percent, Bakongo 13 percent, European 1 percent, *mestico* (mixed European and native African) 2 percent, others 22 percent

MAIN RELIGIONS
Roman Catholic 60 percent, Protestant 17 percent, indigenous beliefs 23 percent (2009 estimate)

LAND USE
Arable land 2.65 percent, permanent crops 0.23 percent, others 97.12 percent (2005 estimate)

RIVERS
Cuanza, Congo, and Cunene

CLIMATE
Semiarid in south and along coast to Luanda; north has cool, dry season (May—October) and hot, rainy season (November—April)

PROVINCES
Bengo, Benguela, Bie, Cabinda, Cuando Cubango, Cuanza Norte, Cuanza Sul, Cunene, Huambo, Huila, Luanda, Lunda Norte, Lunda Sul, Malanje, Moxico, Namibe, Uige, Zaire

BIRTHRATE
43.69 births per 1,000 population (2009 estimate)

DEATH RATE
24.44 deaths per 1,000 population (2008 estimate)

LIFE EXPECTANCY
38.2 years (2009 estimate)

TIME LINE

IN ANGOLA	IN THE WORLD
1300 Kongo kingdom consolidates in the north.	
1483 Portuguese arrive.	**1530** Beginning of transatlantic slave trade organized by the Portuguese in Africa.
1575 Portuguese found Luanda.	
1836 Slave trade officially abolished.	**1789–99** The French Revolution
1885–1930 Portugal consolidates colonial control over Angola.	**1869** The Suez Canal is opened.
1956 The early beginnings of the socialist guerrilla independence movement, the People's Movement for the Liberation of Angola (MPLA).	
1950–1961 Guerrilla war begins.	
1974 Revolution in Portugal; colonial empire collapses.	
1975 Angola gains independence, but a power struggle ensues between the MPLA and the FNLA plus UNITA.	
1979 MPLA leader Agostinho Neto dies. Jose Eduardo dos Santos takes over as president.	
1989 Dos Santos and Unita leader Jonas Savimbi agree to a ceasefire, which collapses soon afterward and guerrilla activity resumes.	
1991 MPLA drops Marxism-Leninism in favor of social democracy. Dos Santos and Savimbi sign peace deal that results in a new multiparty constitution.	**1991** Breakup of the Soviet Union
1992 Presidential and parliamentary polls certified by United Nations monitors as generally free and fair. Dos Santos wins more votes than Savimbi, who rejects the results and resumes guerrilla war.	

IN ANGOLA	IN THE WORLD
1994	
Government and UNITA sign the Lusaka Protocol peace accord.	
1995	
Dos Santos and Savimbi meet and confirm their commitment to peace. The first of 7,000 United Nations peacekeepers arrive.	
1996	
Dos Santos and Savimbi agree to form a unity government and join forces into a national army.	
1997	**1997**
Unified government inaugurated, with Savimbi declining a post in the unity government and failing to attend inauguration ceremony.Tension mounts, with few UNITA troops having integrated into army.	Hong Kong is returned to China.
1998	
Full-scale fighting resumes. A United Nations plane is shot down. Angola intervenes in a civil war in Democratic Republic of Congo on the side of President Laurent-Desire Kabila.	**2001**
2002	Terrorists crash planes into New York, Washington, D.C., and Pennsylvania.
Savimbi killed by government troops. The government and UNITA sign a ceasefire.	
2003	**2003**
President dos Santos appoints Fernando da Piedade Dias dos Santos, as prime minister. UNITA—now a political party—elects Isaias Samakuva as its new leader.	War in Iraq begins.
2007	
President dos Santos says parliamentary elections will be held in 2008 and presidential polls in 2009.	
2008	**2008**
President dos Santos's governing MPLA party scores a landslide victory in the first parliamentary elections in 16 years, winning around 82 percent of the vote. The UNITA party says it will accept the result.	The first black president of the United States, Barack Obama, is elected.

GLOSSARY

afro-montane
A term used to describe the plant and animal species common to the mountains of Africa and the southern Arabian Peninsula.

assimilado (ass-sim-ill-AD-o)
Special status given to Angolans who adopted the Portuguese way of life during colonial rule.

barkcloth
A soft, thick, slightly textured fabric so named because it has a rough surface like that of tree bark.

biome
A large community of plants and animals that occupies a distinct region.

bombom (BOMB-bomb)
Untreated cassava.

caderneta (KAD-er-ne-ta)
Special identity cards carried by Angolans during Portuguese colonial rule.

exclave
An area of land that is part of another country but separated physically from that country.

fetish
Term for describing an object that is worshipped by a people because of a belief in the object's magical or spiritual quality.

gouache
Method of painting that uses opaque pigments ground in water and mixed with a glue-like substance.

kimbanda (kim-BAN-da)
Diviner or witch doctor.

kimberlites
Shafts of volcanic rock known for containing diamonds.

komba (KUM-ba)
Funeral.

intertropical
Occurring between the Tropic of Cancer and the Tropic of Capricorn.

maka (MAR-ka)
African word meaning "problem" that has entered the Portuguese spoken in Angola.

makisi avamala (ma-KI-si a-va-MAR-la)
Masks worn by male dancers of the Mbwela tribe.

masemba (MASS-m-ba)
A type of dance popular in Luanda where a pair of dancers thrust their stomachs toward one another.

musseque (MUS-seek)
Shantytown.

pao burro (pow BORE-o)
Bread popular in smaller towns and in the countryside.

standpipe
A vertical pipe into which water is pumped.

sub-montane
Under or beneath a mountain or mountains.

upwelling
A process in which cold, often nutrient-rich waters from the ocean depths rise to the surface.

FOR FURTHER INFORMATION

BOOKS

Bender, Gerald J. *Angola Under the Portuguese: The Myth and the Reality.* Trenton: Africa World Press, 2004.

Blin, Christopher S. *Swimming to Angola: And Other Tips for Surviving the Third World.* Bloomington: AuthorHouse, 2007.

Cramer, Christopher. *Civil War Is Not a Stupid Thing: Accounting for Violence in Developing Countries.* London: Hurst & Co., 2006.

Gerdes, Paulus. *Drawings from Angola: Living Mathematics.* Lulu.com, 2007.

Hodges, Tony. *Angola: The Anatomy of an Oil State (African Issues).* Bloomington: Indiana University Press, 2003.

Mendes, Pedro Rosa (Author) and Landers, Clifford (Translator). *Bay of Tigers: A Journey Through War-Torn Angola.* London: Granta Books, 2004.

Staeger, Rob. *Angola (Africa: Continent in the Balance).* Broomall: Mason Crest Publishers, 2007.

Wilson, Ernest T. *Angola Beloved.* Port Colborne: Gospel Folio Press, 2007.

WEBSITES

Breaking news from Angola, www.allafrica.com/angola/

CIA World Factbook Angola, www.cia.gov/library/publications/the-world-factbook/geos/ao.html

Infoplease Angola, www.infoplease.com/ipa/A0107280.html

The Embassy of Angola, www.angola.org/

FILMS

Ganga, Maria João. *Hollow City.* First Run Features, DVD, 2006.

Stucke, Mark. *The War Business.* Journeyman Pictures, DVD, 2008.

MUSIC

Grupo de Capoeira Angola Pelourinho: Capoeira Angola, Vol. 2, Brincandoo Na Roda. Smithsonian Folkways, 2003.

Lulendo: Angola. Buda Musique, 2006.

Nzínga: Capoeíra Angola. Tratore Music Brasil, 2004.

BIBLIOGRAPHY

BOOKS

Alden, Chris. *China in Africa: Partner, Competitor or Hegemon? (African Arguments)*. London: Zed Books, 2007.

Berkeley, Bill. *The Graves Are Not Yet Full: Race, Tribe, and Power in the Heart of Africa*. New York, Basic Books, 2001.

Chabal, Patrick; Birmingham, David; Forrest, Joshua; Newitt, Malyn; Seibert, Gerhard and Silva Andrade, Elisa. *A History of Postcolonial Lusophone Africa*. Bloomington: Indiana University Press, 2002.

Clapham, Christopher. *Africa and the International System: The Politics of State Survival (Cambridge Studies in International Relations)*. Cape Town: Cambridge University Press, 2008.

Ghazvinian, John. *Untapped: The Scramble for Africa's Oil*. Orlando: Harvest Books, 2008.

Maier, Karl. *Angola: Promises and Lies. London:* Serif Publishing, 1996.

McKissack, Patricia. *Nzingha: Warrior Queen of Matamba, Angola, Africa, 1595 (The Royal Diaries)*. New York: Scholastic Inc., 2000.

Moorhouse, Karin and Cheng, Wei. *No One Can Stop the Rain: A Chronicle of Two Foreign Aid Workers during the Angolan Civil War*. London: Insomniac Press, 2000.

WEBSITES

Africa Travel Magazine Angola Introduction, www.africa-ata.org/angola_intro.htm

Angola (country) MSN Encarta, http://encarta.msn.com/encyclopedia_761571092_3/Angola_(country).html

Angola Mission Team—Angola at a Glance, http://angolateam.org/angola.html

Encyclopedia of the Nations: Africa: Angola: Media, www.nationsencyclopedia.com/Africa/Angola-MEDIA.html

International Spotlight—Angola, www.washingtonpost.com/wp-adv/specialsales/spotlight/angola/article1.html

One World Angola Guide, http://uk.oneworld.net/guides/angola/development

RUSI Angola comes of age after general elections, www.rusi.org/research/studies/africa/commentary/ref:C48CF8CF4BC4EB/

UN Commission on Status of Women Forty-sixth Session, www.un.org/News/Press/docs/2002/wom1323.doc.htm

UN Office for the Coordination of Humanitarian Affairs—Angola: Humanitarian Country Profile, www.irinnews.org/country.aspx?CountryCode=AO&RegionCode=SAF

UN World Food Programme Angola, www.wfp.org/countries/angola

INDEX

INDEX